I Forgot To Smile

or

How I Was Set Free from

Asperger's Disorder

By

T.S. Cairns

Copyright © 2014 by T.S. Cairns

ISBN: 978-1-888081-16-9

Printed in the United States of America

Published by Good News Ministries
220 Sleepy Creek Rd
Macon GA 31210

Table of Contents

INTRODUCTION

The following testimony is my unique experience and what I am about to relate should not be taken as a formula to follow, but as an encouragement that there is healing.

Much prayer for healing had been received from many individuals, not the least of which was my wife, over the few years between the diagnosis of Asperger's Disorder and my healing and deliverance.

God had been working on my heart for a long time, doing the preparation required in order to receive healing and deliverance. I am still receiving more healing in areas. There are still habit patterns to break and areas to be restored to wholeness.

This book is not a medical document. It is not a thesis on the psychology or spiritual nature of Asperger's Disorder. It is my story.

I have tried to limit the events to those that demonstrate the effect Asperger's has had on my life and on the lives of those around me.

When I write my thoughts, they are often written as I used think when I had Asperger's. They are not describing the way a person normally would think.

If you feel that many of the characteristics I describe in this story relate to you, your partner or child, then consider having them diagnosed by a specialist in Asperger's.

People with Asperger's are at risk of depression and anxiety disorders and may have reached a point where they require medication, but don't realise it.

I also recommend that the person sees a psychologist and is completely honest with them in their answers. Most people I have met with Asperger's are very good at disguising their own problems and pointing to their partners as the cause for their marital issues.

People with Asperger's are experts at presenting circumstances in a way that shows them in the best light and the other person in the worst. I should know, because I was one and when I spoke to my family, Tania, my wife, always came out looking bad.

When I saw my psychologist I made the decision that she would see me behave in the same way as my wife saw me behave. I didn't try to hide anything and so she was able to point out where my behaviours were inappropriate or abusive. I didn't like it, but I did my best to accept it, after I sulked for a week or so.

A psychologist will also help with strategies in coping with the difficulties associated with Asperger's. They can help the person with Asperger's understand themselves better and give them understanding of their partner or other significant family members.

Psychologists can also help those without Asperger's understand the loved one who has it and help them manage it more effectively.

When I look back at my experience I see three ways that Asperger's was tackled. I took the medication required to combat depression and anxiety.

I looked at behaviour modification in order to reduce the emotional and physical effects of Asperger's, including learning communication strategies, and I received spiritual ministry.

In my case, none of those would have been effective on their own. The reason for this is because, in my opinion, Asperger's is a mix of both physical and spiritual causes.

My wife and I once prayed for our son, who was also diagnosed with Asperger's. We prayed specifically in the spiritual arena. Many of the behavioural issues disappeared, including emotional meltdowns.

A little while after, Caleb complained that his hearing wasn't as good. He couldn't hear conversations all around like he used to. He said he didn't like his hearing like it was and he wanted it back the old way. Not long after that, his hypersensitive hearing returned and so did the behavioural issues.

If you have Asperger's and you want healing, then you are probably looking for the "Six Steps to Healing." It won't work. There are no six steps; there is only what God wants to do in your life and how He wants to do it.

I know that's hard to grasp, but it's the truth. You are unique. You have not had the same experiences as me. You do not have the same family generational line as I do.

This testimony is to give you hope, not to give you the steps to follow. You will benefit from Sozo ministry, or a similar ministry that gets to roots and generational roots; How it looks for you or what is exposed will be different and the effect it has on you will be different. What I can guarantee is that God wants to heal you and He can heal you.

I can trace my healing and deliverance journey back fifteen years before there was a dramatic change. I didn't even know I needed healing when God first started the process, but the little steps along the way opened the door for the bigger steps that needed to occur. There is hope for you and those that you love.

A diagnosis of Asperger's does not have to set the prognosis in stone. God loves you and He wants you to be able to function in the fullness He designed you for. Yes, it is possible to manage the difficulties associated with Asperger's Disorder (and in truth, some people thrive), but I believe that managed Asperger's is settling for second place in terms of how God wants you to enjoy His plan for your life.

ABOUT THE AUTHOR

Tim Cairns and his wife, Tania, have been married for fourteen years. Together, they pastor two churches in the Hunter Valley, New South Wales, Australia, where they live with their their son Caleb. Their two daughters, Shantelle and Candice, are grown and Shantelle and her husband are expecting their first child. Tim was previously a science teacher, where he was responsible for several school evacuations after blowing things up in laboratory experiments gone wrong.

Tim tried many avenues to help God bring finances into the kingdom. He soon discovered that his gifting lay in other areas and in fact, God didn't actually need his help. He has been leading ministries in churches for nearly twenty years and finds it is more successful and less stressful when he just does what God tells him to do.

Tim enjoys writing and has other publications listed on www.scorebrowniepoints.com.au with more to come. The website is dedicated to exploring grace in relationships with our spouse and with God.

PART 1 - I FORGOT TO SMILE

CHAPTER 1

"Mr. No Smiley"

It was a name I was given by students in the schools I taught at. They would often ask why I never smiled. I made up all kinds of reasons but the truth was that I never knew.

In 2010 I was diagnosed with Asperger's Disorder (or Syndrome). After some time with a psychologist I found out why I didn't smile. It was simply because I forgot.

Forgot to smile? That must seem like one of the most nonsensical things to ever be put into print. You don't have to remember to smile. You just do.

Smiling, interpreting body language, understanding the nuances of language, relating to people in a socially acceptable manner are things that happen instinctively with people as they grow older. The part of the brain in charge of social understanding develops and interactions with people can run on autopilot. A person with Asperger's doesn't develop in that part of their brain. They don't have an autopilot for social responses.

A person with Asperger's will use and rehearse responses that they develop over time. If there is a favourable response from a script then they will use it again, and again. They may tell the same joke to the same people every time they meet. If they get a negative response, the script will be dropped and a new script found.

Of course there are times when a script is appropriate for one setting, but not another. A person with Asperger's will be very confused when the script they have used with great success in one setting receives a negative response in another setting.

Once, as a student in my later years at High School, I was asked how my day had been. I gave my regular response, which was to relate the events of my day from the time I got up to the time right then, nearly home time. This worked at home. It didn't work at school. The fellow student who asked me said, "I asked how your day was. I didn't ask for your life story."

To me it was an unpleasant experience. I did however learn that relating a whole day's events was an inappropriate response so I modified my answer to questions like that.

I made some new scripts. I said something along the lines of "Great (smile). How has your day been (tilt head a little, turn ear slightly toward speaker, raise eyebrows a little, pretend to be interested in response)?" It worked quite well most of the time.

When teaching, there was constant interaction and often times conflict with students. The classrooms were not that quiet and I was always on guard during practical Science lessons. I was watching what all the students were doing all the time, and was constantly assaulted by the movement and sound in and out of the classroom.

I suppose if I was to conjure up a scenario that might have a similar effect on someone not on the Autism Spectrum it might be like sitting at a desk in the middle of a disco roller skating rink, full of roller skating people (with disco lights flashing and disco music blaring at full volume) trying to do three different quantum physics exams written in a foreign language.

Throughout the day I had been focusing so hard on managing the classroom and teaching the required syllabus that I wasn't able to concentrate on the socially acceptable "norm" of emotional engagement. In other words, I forgot to smile.

PART 2 - I HAD ASPERGER'S

CHAPTER 2

The psychologist confirmed what I had found on the internet. In 2010, my wife had suggested that my son might have Asperger's so I researched it.

When I saw the symptoms of Asperger's I recognised a lot of them in myself. We went to the psychologist and she diagnosed us. She also gave us the prognosis.

There is no cure!

I was born with it. I would die with it. The best I could hope for was to find strategies that would help me manage it.

Asperger's is recognised as being part of the Autism Spectrum. It is associated with social anxiety that often leads to depression.

A person with Asperger's will often not recognise the physical or emotional symptoms of anxiety or depression, so identification will require a list of behaviours associated with those issues.

Asperger's might not kill the carrier physically, but it can wreck them emotionally, it can destroy their relationships, it can isolate them socially and it can mess up their view of themselves, others and God.

The scariest thing about it is that I didn't even realise it was doing just that to me.

The psychologist told me that I was high functioning in terms of Asperger's. High functioning Asperger's basically means that it is easier to hide the differences between neuro-typical and neuro-atypical behaviours.

The psychologist also said that most marriages between men with Asperger's and women without it lasted about five years. The fact that my wife and I were still married after ten years was a testament to God's goodness. While my ability to hide the abnormality may have helped keep our marriage going, it was my wife's desire to make the marriage last that really made the difference.

My wife and I had just received the leadership of a church when I was diagnosed with Asperger's. I was learning new skills, I was tired and stressed and my thinking went into what the psychologist called default mode.

Being high functioning, I was able to cover up my real thought processes for most of the time.

When I was placed under high stress, constantly changing circumstances or I didn't sleep enough, my thought processes were exposed and I wasn't able to moderate them with prepared scripts. I wasn't able to think through the situation and say what would be reasonable or socially acceptable.

We had a little dog called Cindy. I put her outside to go to the toilet before we all went to bed.

Because I hadn't been sleeping well, I had gone into default mode in my thinking.

I had the dog outside for nearly forty five minutes, because I knew, without a shadow of doubt that she was going to poo inside the house that night, because we hadn't given her enough attention. I could just tell that she was plotting revenge.

My wife thought it was funny. I told her she wouldn't think it was funny when she was cleaning up the poo, because I sure as heck wasn't going to do it.

Of course the dog didn't poo and the next morning, after a good sleep, I couldn't work out why I thought the way I had. I was out-rightly paranoid.

The big problem with this paranoia was that it permeated my relationships, particularly with my wife. I just assumed that things she said were designed to hurt me. That she purposefully did things because she knew I wouldn't like them.

In my mind, Tania never considered my perspective and that everything was about her. It was killing our marriage. I was killing our marriage.

PART 3 - AN ASPERGER'S MIND

What does Asperger's look like? The following is a description that might give a better understanding. While this specific event did not happen, it combines events that did occur at other times.

CHAPTER 3

The morning had been the best I could hope for. I re-read the last paragraph I had written on a fictional story I occasionally worked on. I deleted a word and replaced it with a better one. I sighed with content, ready to start typing the next paragraph.

I had played an hour of Spider Solitaire and then written for two hours.

I looked out the kitchen window at the clear morning sky. I would have to mow the lawn today and I hated mowing. It hurt my ears and the vibrations felt bad and I would rather be writing.

But it was Saturday and Saturday was Lawn Mowing Day.

I was glad my wife was sleeping late. I didn't want to wake her up to the sound of a lawn mower and so I would have to delay it. That's what I would want if I slept that late. But I can't sleep late. It's too light and the kids down the road start playing and making noise. Then the dogs down the road bark at the kids.

My wife should know I can't sleep late. I always get up early. She knows that. She should come to bed earlier so I can get to sleep earlier. I keep telling her I'm tired.

I looked back at my work and tried to tune out the rising anger. If she really loved me she would come to bed earlier and let me get the sleep I need. The psychologist told her I need to get lots of sleep, so she does know that. Oh, that's right. This is her cycle.

We'd been getting along well lately, even been intimate and now she's pushing me away. It happens every time. So much for love well and be loved! I treat her better than most husbands treat their wives.

I know she's been in counselling dealing with 'issues' but she's been having it for ages and nothing changes. I don't see why I should have to pay for her wrong doing.

My son got up and turned the TV on in the lounge room up a short flight of stairs.

"Turn it down Caleb," I called quietly up the stairs. "Don't wake up your mum."

I looked back at my laptop screen trying to focus but I couldn't remember what I was writing. I went back to Spider Solitaire to refocus. I won a game, moved back to the story and started typing.

CHAPTER 4

The bed creaks. Tania is up.

She opened up my side of the cupboard and the sliding door bangs sharply against another slider. I knew it was my side because she keeps her dressing gowns in my side of the cupboard. Plus she arranged the doors wrong. If she arranged them the way I do, they wouldn't bang like that and the bang hurts my ears. I don't know why she hadn't noticed that. I changed the doors around enough.

She'll probably be wearing the white, fluffy dressing gown with the pink flowers. It seemed to be her favourite at the moment. Plus she left the other winter dressing gown on the ground in the lounge room. I saw it this morning and thought I'll probably have to pick it up later.

Tania walked out of the bedroom, down the hall and into the kitchen, still tying the dressing gown. Her slippers scuff across the tiles.

"Morning," She said.

"Morning," I replied.

"How cold was it last night?" She said.

"The news said it would get down to minus two degrees Celsius but I haven't checked what it really reached last night. I can check if you want?" I replied.

"No," Tania answered. "I don't want to know."

I nearly replied that if she didn't want to know, she shouldn't ask but I remembered that "How cold was it last night" can be a statement about it being very cold, not a question about how cold it was.

I remember someone saying that in school and when I replied that I hadn't read the news, everyone laughed and said it was a good joke. I didn't know it was a joke, but I kept listening over time for similar comments and finally worked out what they meant.

CHAPTER 5

I was trying to shift mental boxes. I was still in the "writing" box and I had to change to the "talking with people" box or I could make more silly mistakes. It takes a bit of time, changing boxes.

"Did you sleep well?" I asked Tania. That seemed like a good start and the beginning of a script that has worked well in the past. I looked at her face, dropped my arms to the side of the chair and began to rotate my fists around and around. Maintain eye contact. It's important.

I hadn't liked starting conversations with Tania for a while. I didn't know where they might go. I didn't have scripts for everything Tania might say. I hadn't learned the right words yet.

I opened my fists and began to touch the tips of each of my fingers to the thumb of each hand. Index, Middle, Ring, Pinkie. Ring, Middle, Index.

Middle, Ring, Pinkie. First one way and then the other. 1, 2, 3, 4. 1, 2, 3. 1, 2, 3.

"Mostly," she replied. "You touched me a few times with your arm through the night and I could feel the cold of it through my pyjamas. It was so cold it woke me up. Why don't you wear something warmer to bed?"

I'd had on my boxers and a tee-shirt. I thought it was warm. "What I've got on is comfortable," I replied.

Tania shook her head, moved to the bench and turned on the kettle.

"Aren't you cold?" She asked me.

"I don't think so," I answered. I'm not aware of feeling cold. I could be but I haven't taken the time to look for the signs. Shivering, goose bumps, slight blue colouring around the toes and fingers. "I could be."

"I'm sure you are," Tania sighed. "Go put your track pants and Ugg Boots on."

I stood up to go and Tania said something else. I didn't understand what she said.

"What was that?" I asked her.

"I asked you if you've had breakfast yet," she replied. "How could you not hear me? I'm standing right next to you."

"The kettle boiled at the same time you spoke. That, combined with the TV and Caleb flushing the toilet, my scraping chair, the barking dog from the house two doors down, the lawn mower next door, the whipper snipper from across the road and the motorbike riding past the kid on his bike with the clacky noise maker on his wheels made it difficult to hear. Plus you turned away to look at the kettle so I couldn't match the sounds with your lips to try and get it to make sense." I replied.

"What …?" Tania began to ask but stopped, all the sounds her mind had automatically blocked out assaulting her senses as I mentioned the cause of them.

"Anyway," Tania continued. "What did you have for breakfast?"

"I haven't had breakfast," I said. "I didn't think about eating. I was busy on my computer and I forgot."

"You'd forget your head if it wasn't screwed on. You need to have breakfast," Tania stated. I paused while I processed Tania's statements. I remember the first time I heard Tania's initial statement. Mum said it to me when I was young. I was scared until she explained that my head is not really screwed on and that I couldn't leave it anywhere by accident.

Anyway, why was she having a go about me forgetting something? She's got no right to say anything to me about forgetting food when she was meant to bring lunch down to the church to me about a year ago and she forgot to bring it. It was the only time I'd asked her to as well.

She's smiling at me. Did she mean that as a joke? I don't know. I thought about the second statement. Which would be more important to Tania for me to do? Eating breakfast or getting warmer clothes.

I was getting up to put on warmer clothes but she stopped me and told me I need to have breakfast. What if I did one first and she expected me to do the other? What if I get it wrong? Would she be angry? Which would make her happier and therefore make my life easier? I took a guess and went to the pantry.

CHAPTER 6

"Where are you going?" Tania asked.

"To the pantry to get breakfast," I replied.

"Go and get some warm clothes on."

I got it wrong, but it's not my fault.

"You told me to get breakfast," I said, defending myself against the attack.

"What? No I didn't," was the retort.

"Yes you did. You said that I needed to have breakfast."

"No, I said that you should remember to have breakfast every morning so that you won't get hungry and fill up on junk."

"No! Don't lie. You didn't say that. You said I needed to have breakfast. Those were the words."

"Those may have been the words but when you put everything together that was not the meaning."

"But that's what you said."

"But that's not what they meant."

"Then say what you mean. I can't read your mind. How am I supposed to know that what you actually said was not what you were meaning? When I say things I mean what I say. It's not too hard you know. You just stop speaking long enough not to let garbage come out. You ought to try it."

"What's wrong? How come you're so upset?"

"I don't want to talk about it. I'm going to go mow the lawn."

"Tim, we need to be able to talk about things."

"I told you, I don't want to. There's nothing wrong with me."

"What is going on? We can't keep this marriage working if we don't talk."

"Oh, you want to know what's going on? Alright, I'll tell you," I said, rounding on Tania.

The way she shrank back from me must have meant my eyes were bulging. She always said bulging eyes meant I was manifesting. I got angrier thinking about it.

Adrenaline flowed into my system and my body swelled to make me look bigger and more intimidating. I knew she was scared, although she would never admit it.

I could only feel anger and I couldn't temper it with love. Tania said she could be angry with me and still love me. I couldn't. I could only feel one thing at a time, and at this time it was anger.

"I was having a good morning until you came out here with your accusations," I said.

"Accusations? What are you talking about? What accusations?" Tania butted in.

"What accusations?" I stated, raising my voice. "You stand there accusing me of destroying our marriage and you ask me about accusations? I do everything I can for this marriage. I am always doing things for you. It's never enough. You're never satisfied. You should have married

Superman. He's the only one who could measure up to your demands."

"You tell me I'm wrecking the marriage," I continued. "But you don't even care enough to listen to the psychologist and do what she says to do. You know I need to get sleep but you don't care. All you care about is how to get out of having sex with me. That's why you stayed up late, wasn't it?" "You accused me of being forgetful," I raged. "And yet you are the one who forgot to bring me food, the only time I ever asked you to do it. Talk? I can't talk to you. You don't listen to me anyway. You just want to say what you want to say and won't listen when I talk. Your talking involves you running me down, you telling me what's wrong with me and me not being able to say anything about it. I don't want to talk to you."

I turned around to head off to the bedroom to get changed. As I went I saw the tears forming in Tania's eyes. I turned back.

"Now you're crying," I said. "See? This is why I tell you not to push me to talk with you when I say I'm not going to. You always do this. You forced me to say something and I hadn't had time to work out how to say it without hurting you. If you had just let it go, I wouldn't have said that the way I did and you wouldn't have got hurt. You need to listen to me."

I turned around and went to the bedroom to the sound of Tania's sobbing. Another day had turned bad.

Why couldn't she just leave things as they were? Why did she have to keep pushing me? Why couldn't she just learn how to understand me and how to talk to me properly? Why couldn't she just work with what I need? Marriage is a two way thing and she needs to give too. Our marriage could work if only she could see what she needed to do for her part.

PART 4 - CHILDHOOD

CHAPTER 7

As a boy I was obsessed with bugs. I played with them all the time. I would get books about them and memorize their names. I would burn them using a magnifying glass. I would feed them to ants or stick them in spider webs.

I would pull the legs or wings off the bugs and then drop them in an ants nest or burn them. I would put them in jars together and watch them fight. When I walked home from school I would often be late because I would stop and follow ant trails back to their nests.

I loved lighting fires. I daydreamed. I made up stories and lived in a fantasy world. I didn't have many friends. I preferred to spend my time sitting in my room reading rather than being outside playing (unless it was with bugs).

I would make up new uses for words. There was the "Rain Often Day," because it would rain off 'n' on all day. When I walked slowly, I would be just "snailing along." To me, that was normal and I assumed every other boy was the same. Apparently it's not normal to torture bugs and want to light fires.

I tried to tell my wife that it was normal for boys to do that when my son started doing similar things. My brother and his sons had also done the same thing. It was normal.

There was nothing wrong with my son when he pulled a sharp piece of glass out of a broken picture frame and began to repeatedly stab the blow up pool we had because it made interesting sounds.

I was sure there was nothing abnormal about it even though he continued stabbing the pool after he had cut his own hand with the glass. It was something I would do, so all boys must be the same.

My wife didn't think it was normal and she was right. I did however convince her that our son would not do the same thing to our dog as he did to the pool. At least I was right about that.

CHAPTER 8

We played wars at school. It would involve me hiding in the long grass down an embankment. The other boys in the class would throw rocks at me while I tried to make my way up to the top. While I didn't like being hit by rocks, the boys at school would at least play with me.

One time I slashed my leg open on a rusty tin can and had to get it stitched up. Because of the injury, the teachers found out about the game and put a stop to it. I didn't understand why.

The boys at school seemed to find some respect for me because when I got up and walked up the hill, with blood pouring down my leg, I wasn't crying. I was only six years old and they all thought I was tough.

Dad used to call me "Butch" because of that. It didn't mean then what it means now. Back then it just meant "tough". I seldom reacted to physical pain; which was good, because I hurt myself a lot.

CHAPTER 9

I was un-coordinated and regularly had accidents. My mum would say that even though I was the quietest and least adventurous of all the children, I was the one most likely to end up in hospital. And I did.

One time, when I was eight years old, I was exploring how a washing machine wringer worked and I got my finger caught in it. I didn't know what to do. If I let my hand go through the wringer, it might smash the brand new watch I had. I wasn't strong enough to pull it back out so I just held it there.

I apparently squeaked like a guinea pig. Since we had guinea pigs nobody noticed until the noise went on for a while. Eventually Mum sent my little sister down to find out why the guinea pigs were still making so much noise. She found me instead. She got Mum and Dad's attention more successfully than I did. They rushed me to hospital and the result of my unsupervised exploration was a third degree friction burn that required a skin graft. I don't remember crying. .

I cried when I had the cast cut off because the sound the machine made hurt my ears and I was scared. I also cried when they tried to remove the yellow gauze from the skin graft because the graft had grown through the gauze and they were ripping the skin off trying to remove it. In fact that experience was so traumatic for me, that twenty years later it came back to haunt me.

At twenty eight years old I was a one hundred kilo Rugby Union prop. I was solid and strong. I had broken bones, been cut up by steel studs on boots and been in fights on the field. I hadn't flinched when I had an infected tooth removed with no anesthetic. I made jokes when a doctor tried to reset a broken finger after shoving the needle right through the webbing of my hand and squirting the anesthetic on the floor.

During a game someone had trodden on my foot and twisted, breaking my big toe and causing bleeding under my toenail. After about two weeks of hobbling around and watching my toenail swell up and turn black, I thought I'd better go to the doctor's. I watched with interest as the doctor removed the toenail. When the doctor came out with yellow gauze to put over the place where my toenail had been, I started to panic. I nearly cried when I told him I didn't want the yellow gauze. I told him I'd have anything but that, just don't make me have the yellow gauze.

I don't think the doctor was expecting the reaction he got after seeing me so calmly watch the operation. The problem was that I had only one experience with yellow gauze and I wasn't capable of imagining a different one.

A person with Asperger's finds it very hard to imagine how experiences will feel unless they have been through them. Once they have been through that experience, it gets locked in their mind. That is what it feels like, it will be the same every time and it is the same for everybody else.

I had a psychologist tell me it can be helpful to anticipate feelings of certain events to help with resilience. He said he sometimes allows himself to feel what it might be like to lose one of his parents. Not for long and not morbidly but it helps prepare for something that will eventually happen.

I was not able to do that because it hadn't actually happened. This is why people with Asperger's do not have true empathy.

If someone goes through an experience similar to one the person with Asperger's has gone through, they can project how they felt in that situation onto the other person. They will assume that everyone will feel the same, because that is how they felt and they can't imagine anyone feeling any different.

When a person with Asperger's doesn't react to someone else's emotional situation, it is usually not because they don't care, but because they don't understand.

CHAPTER 10

At the primary school I went to there was almost a junior and middle school situation. There were toilets allocated to the older children and they were different to the ones the younger children used.

I reached ten years old, and I had to start using the bigger kid's toilets. That was OK until some bigger kids found me using them.

These kids were around twelve years old, maybe even thirteen. They told me that I was not to use the toilets there again. If I did, they would flush my head down the toilet. That was particularly scary for me. I had seen what got flushed down the toilet and I didn't want my head going to the same place.

The other problem was that I had been held under the water before at a swimming pool and experience told me that it wasn't pleasant.

I went back to using the small kid's toilets, but a teacher found me and told me never to use those toilets again. I had to use the big kid's toilets.

I knew I had to do what my teachers told me. Mum and Dad had been very clear about that. I couldn't use the toilets for the big kids because the big kids had been very clear about that.

During a lesson I would ask to go to the toilet and I would walk backward and forward between the toilets not knowing what to do, too scared to use either of them. Eventually I would just wet myself. I would go back to class and get in trouble from the teacher for being away from class too long.

The teacher held me back one day and asked me what was happening. I told her and she said I could use the small kid's toilets until the next year. I was worried about what the other teachers would say, but I didn't get into trouble again so it was OK. The next year I used the big kid's toilets.

CHAPTER 11

The next year was an interesting one. I discovered my third great hate. The first two hates were Brussels sprouts and Cauliflower. They would make me vomit when I tried to eat them. My third great hate was craft.

The problem I had was that my teacher that year loved craft. He was always, "Let's make this" or "Let's make that." I wouldn't know what to do. I couldn't imagine ways to make things.

My hands wouldn't do what I wanted them to do. I couldn't colour in between lines, cut straight lines, draw pictures or even write well. It was a consistent comment all through school. "Tim needs to improve his handwriting." I never could though, no matter how hard I tried.

I kept asking my teacher what to do and how to do it. All the time, every day, multiple times through the day. He never gave me specific enough answers though so I kept asking. Eventually he must have said something like, "Go and amuse yourself while I help this other student." So I did. I went outside to play on the play gym.

I would spend a long time playing there amusing myself. At some point in time other students noticed and came out as well. I was disappointed because I liked having the play gym to myself. I didn't have to touch anyone, there wasn't much noise and I didn't have to try to make conversation. I could play or I could make up stories. No-one interrupted me.

I thought about asking the teacher to tell the other students to, "Go amuse themselves somewhere else," but then he might decide that none of us could amuse ourselves on the play gym.

The play gym time didn't last too many weeks as one of the other students fell off the gym and broke his arm. I was pretty annoyed with him for spoiling my fun. It was a lot better than craft.

That year, I also discovered that I was strong. I could beat all my class in arm wrestles. When we played games that involved hitting each other in the arm, I never flinched. My classmates stopped teasing me and I started making friends. People from other classes did tease me though, and one day I snapped.

I remember starting to run after the person who was teasing me, although I don't know why because I was not a fast runner. I "saw red" and the next thing I knew, there were three or four people dragging me off the other boy.

I had apparently chased the older boy, tackled him, sat on top of him, grabbed his head and started bashing it into the ground. It was soft ground so he wasn't hurt but no-one really gave me a hard time after that. In fact, there weren't many people who had anything to do with me after that.

There was this one girl though, who kept trying to beat me in an arm wrestle. I was the only boy she couldn't beat. She kept saying that I had to let her win or she would kiss me. Then she changed it and said the first rule still counts but then if she won, I had to kiss her. I didn't like her forcing me to lose so I stopped arm wrestling her. I didn't like losing.

The "seeing red" thing had happened once before. When I was a couple of years younger I had a play fight with a son in a family my parents had invited around. I was told to play with him because he was my age. He wanted to play fight but I didn't.

We weren't allowed to fight at our house. He started hitting me anyway. I stood there and told him not to hit me. He said that it was just a play fight. I said that we don't hit each other if we have play fights. He kept hitting me and I told him to stop. I showed him how to swing and miss but he kept hitting me. I didn't understand how he didn't get it.

I told him not to hit me again or I wouldn't play. He said sorry and then hit me again. By this time he was hitting me in the face.

I started to walk away and he said sorry again and then said he wouldn't hit me anymore, so I turned back. He hit me in the face again and I "saw red." When the red mist cleared he was crying and there was blood running out of his mouth. One of his teeth was missing.

I knew I would get in trouble, we weren't allowed to fight in the house. I knew the rules and I broke them. I started to cry too.

Later, the boy's father said not to worry about it, the tooth was probably loose anyway. I wasn't crying because I had hurt the boy, I was crying because I had broken a rule and would get punished. I don't think the family came back to the house.

CHAPTER 12

I didn't want to hurt people. Mum and Dad had made it very clear that hurting people was naughty and if I was naughty, Dad would get angry, smack me and not talk to me. He wouldn't like me and I wanted him to like me so I tried not to be naughty.

Unless someone told me what was naughty and what wasn't though, I wouldn't know. I had nothing on the inside of me telling me what was good and what was naughty.

I tried to pay close attention to what Dad said were the rules and follow them to the letter. I was very good at following rules. Dad was very good with rules too. If he made a rule, everyone had to follow it. No excuses. Not even for Mum.

We had a set time to eat. We had set places at the table. We had set bed times. We had set times we were allowed to talk when the TV was on and set times not to talk. We had a set day to have take-away for tea and a set take-away to eat. We had a set order for when we were on chores.

There were rules and times for everything. That was fine by me because nothing was a surprise. Not even lunch. Devon sandwiches. That was my favourite.

We began making our own school lunches quite early and that was fine with me, because I made my lunch just the way I liked it.

Mum and Dad had both tried making my lunch but neither of them could do it right. There was either too much butter or not enough; too much sauce or not enough. They would put the Devon in the wrong place. It had to sit right in the middle of the sandwich. I didn't like it when one bit hung too far over the side of the bread.

Sometimes, though, I wouldn't understand a rule and I'd break it. Dad wouldn't like me for a while so I'd try hard by following the rules to get him to like me again. I wouldn't do what I did before, even if I still didn't know what I'd done wrong or why it was wrong.

CHAPTER 13

I gave my life to Jesus when I was eight years old. It was one of the few times I remember being happy. Jesus was my friend. I liked Him and I knew he liked me.

The problem I had was that all my experiences with Dad told me that if I was naughty, then Jesus wouldn't like me because He was a man too. I had new rules to learn and follow because I didn't want Jesus to think I was naughty and not like me. I really wanted Him to like me.

I was good at following the words of the rules, even if I didn't know the meaning behind the rules or why I should follow them. I was very literal. When I was eleven years old, our family moved from New Zealand to Australia.

I started a new school and had to get used to new teachers. One teacher had us lined up outside of the classroom. He told us to go in and take our seats. I went in, picked up a chair and asked him where he wanted us to take it to. The class thought it was really funny. The teacher gave me my first ever detention. I didn't mean to be funny, I wanted to help.

When I thought about it after, if I admitted I hadn't meant it to be funny, people would think I was stupid and I wouldn't want that. I became very good at using literalism as humour, that way, if I made a mistake people wouldn't notice.

I messed up in high school though when I had an exam asking a question about Kenneth Slessor's poem "Five Visions of Captain Cook."

There is a stanza in it speaking of Joseph Bank's wonder over the coral of the Great Barrier Reef. The question asked why "Banks, in all his books on botany, couldn't find a Latin for this loveliness."

I answered literally and was very upset when I received no marks for it. Apparently the answer was meant to include a waxing lyrical about the beauty of coral.

My answer included two facts. 1) Coral had not yet been discovered and so could not have been given a taxonomic name in Latin. 2) Coral is actually an animal and so wouldn't be found in a plant book even if it had been discovered.

While my answer was right, it was still wrong: a fact that I have found to be true in many cases, even when I didn't understand. In my view, if I was right, I was right. If I was wrong, I was wrong. If I'm right, I couldn't be wrong at the same time. I now see that the state of being right and wrong at the same time is not just possible, but quite common.

PART 5 - HIGH SCHOOL

CHAPTER 14

Most of my High School years were in a small Christian School. People got used to my peculiarities. I was also big enough not to have too many people give me a hard time.

During High School, while I loved reading science fiction/ fantasy books, and I enjoyed writing creative fiction, I found my interests turning more toward Maths and Science.

I had a good memory and I could work out fairly complex ideas quite easily. I did comparatively well in Maths and Science, but English became difficult.

I didn't like trying to understand poetry. I didn't enjoy having to interpret novels. The books I read had no underlying, hidden meanings. I didn't have to think about it. I read them and the actions just appeared in my head. It was simple.

I found it hard trying to understand complex human emotions. Why would I even think that the colour of the sky described in a book might be reflective of the main character's mood? When I read a poem, it was supposed to elicit some kind of emotion that I had to describe.

'How does this make you feel' was not a great question to me. I really only had a few emotions I recognised. I knew happy, sad, angry, surprised and afraid. Everything else was "nothing". It wasn't that I didn't feel anything, it was just that I didn't know what it was. I wasn't emotionless. I didn't understand emotions and I couldn't express them appropriately.

"How does it make you feel?" asked the teacher.

"I don't know," I replied.

"How could you not know? Think about it. It's not good enough. Try harder. Tell me! How does it make you feel?" the teacher pestered.

"Angry," I answered.

"Anger is a good start, but the answer should be indignation. Indignation at the injustice suffered by that race," the teacher corrected."

"Well I feel angry," I replied.

"Anger does nothing. Indignation stirs you to action. The author wanted people to be stirred into action and stop the injustice and cruelty, so she wrote the piece specifically to make people feel indignant. If you get a question about this piece in your exam, the word is indignant. Now let's look at how they created that feeling."

"Well I must be indignant then, because I'm feeling stirred into the action of punching you in the head," I thought quietly. Of course I wouldn't hit a teacher. Hitting people was hurting people and Jesus wouldn't like me if I hurt people.

What did it matter to me anyway about people who lived a hundred years ago? I wasn't there. It wasn't me doing it. Those people weren't real to me. Why would I feel indignant or even angry about things that had nothing to do with me or I could do nothing about?

CHAPTER 15

I did the World Vision 40 Hour famine once when I was in High School. I had visions of me raising lots of money and getting prizes. I was going to be famous. Apparently some people would be helped by it too. I didn't raise enough money to get prizes or be famous and I got really hungry too, so I didn't do it again.

I saw images of starving people on TV and it was very rare for me to be stirred by those images. It wasn't that I didn't care; it was that they weren't real to me. Even in High School it seemed to me that if I didn't know someone, they weren't real.

I understood cognitively that people lived in other countries but I couldn't connect emotionally with any of them. I had never had a personal experience with them or what they went through. The closest I had come to that was finishing the 40 Hour Famine, but I completely missed the point of that. I simply couldn't relate to them.

Most people, as they get past the age of five or six develop beyond ego-centric thinking. Ego-centrism is not arrogance. It is the kind of thinking that assumes that I am at the centre of the lives of everyone I know.

A person with Asperger's does not grow out of it. It assumes that if you meet someone new, they must know your friends and family because they are now a part of your circle.

The thought that I might actually be a very minor part of someone else's life never entered my head. I was the centre of my world and so it must be the same for everyone else.

I didn't mean to be self centred, in fact I did my best to think of others first. Jesus wanted me to do that and I wanted Him to keep liking me. I just thought about them from my perspective, not theirs.

It was an incredible surprise to me when I realised for the first time that there may be 4 billion conversations going on at the present time, and not one of them involved me.

It may seem like a selfish attitude but I didn't deliberately adopt it. I didn't know any different. Slapping me and telling me not to be selfish wasn't going to help. Telling me to grow up and consider other people wasn't going to develop that part of my brain.

I honestly wanted to be good. I wanted to please my teachers, my parents and most of all Jesus. I desperately wanted people to like me and I couldn't understand why they didn't.

During High School I tried to adopt a number of different personas to gain approval, but nothing worked. I wanted to fit in, but there was always something different about me. People weren't unkind or mean to me, I just didn't have many people I thought would be close friends.

More than likely, this was my own perspective, insecurity, low self-esteem and my introversion speaking. I may have pushed people away by my actions or in fact, I did actually have lots of friends and I didn't know it. One thing I was certain of though was that girls had absolutely no interest in me.

PART 6 - GIRLS

CHAPTER 16

I wanted a girlfriend. I wanted to be liked. I wanted to be normal. I wanted to feel like someone thought I was special. Not good reasons for forming a relationship that I hoped would last until marriage. I knew there were certain things that I just couldn't do if I had a girlfriend, because if I did, Jesus wouldn't like me. I wanted a girlfriend anyway.

What I found was that there was no-one interested. My younger sister bullied a couple of girls into going out with me, but they quickly broke off the relationship.

What I experienced during those times was proof that people with Asperger's do have feelings. I hurt.

There were girls at school that I liked who developed relationships with other boys from my class. They would get hurt and then come to me to pour all their pain out. I would talk to them and make them feel better, and then they would go out with that same person or another just like them.

I was a natural at not showing my feelings when talking with them. I was good at pretending to be interested when they started sharing the feelings they had for people who weren't me.

For some reason I developed a reputation for being a good listener and being very wise with my advice. I even had guys coming and talking to me during the day as well. Mostly I looked interested, nodded my head and asked them what they thought and "how did you feel about that."

I believe that during that time though, God developed a gift on my life. I counsel people very well and that is unusual for a person with Asperger's.

During some "counseling sessions," there would be a thought that would run across my mind and it would say, "This is the problem." I would say what I heard and it would cut to the heart of the issue. Usually I wouldn't even know why. I would just hear what to say and say it. When it worked like that I knew it had nothing to do with me.

CHAPTER 17

When I look back at my life and my experiences with relationships I have to think that part of my problem was a complete naivety when it came to picking up signals of interest.

In my second last year of High School a new girl started attending the school in my class. She became the interest of most males in my year.

The boys began pinching her on her backside. I was not really keen on contact with people but everyone else was doing it so I joined in. She seemed like a friendly girl so I spent quite a bit of time chatting with her.

That year, at the school athletics carnival, the girl came up to meet my mum and talked with her for a while. They seemed to have a nice conversation. When the girl left I heard my mother mutter,

"There is no way I'm going to let that girl dig her claws into my son."

I don't think I was meant to hear what my mum said but my hearing was very good. At seventeen years of age, unbelievably I had no idea what my mother was talking about.

On another day when I was talking to the girl, she informed me that she didn't like the boys pinching her. She also didn't like it when they came and sat on her butt when she was lying along the bench we sat on. I told her that I would have a word to the boys and they would stop it.

She thanked me and then told me that she didn't mind if I pinched her if I wanted too, or if I used her butt as a cushion. I told her that of course I wouldn't do it. She had told me she didn't like it and I was certainly not going to do anything that she didn't like.

She assured me that she would be completely OK if I pinched her. I was quick to allay her obvious concern that I might take advantage of the fact that I had protected her and I wouldn't do anything she didn't like. I must have been in my mid-thirties before I figured out what she was really saying.

I don't regret not understanding though. While I felt a great sense of rejection and inadequacy through my teen years, I can look back and see how God used my lack of understanding to protect me from even more emotional pain.

Now I am married to the woman of my dreams and I can't imagine how much more baggage I would have brought into our relationship if I had been more able to understand social interactions.

PART 7 – WORK

CHAPTER 18

I spent four years at university learning to be a Science Teacher. My marks at Uni, like school, were average. It didn't matter how hard I tried, I only got average marks.

I thought I was pretty average in most things. It surprised me when I later did an online IQ test and found out I had an IQ of 155.

Some group called Mensa sent me a message at the end of the test asking me for my email address because they wanted me to join them. I didn't know who they were and I had completed the test during time off at work, using work computers. I got scared and shut down the computer in case someone was tracking it.

Later that day I went home and spent nearly ten minutes with my hand under a running tap waiting for the water to warm up. It didn't warm up so I checked the fuses and the hot water cylinder and everything seemed to be working.

I went back to the tap and tried it again but it was still cold. I was considering who I would have to call to get it fixed when I realised I had the tap turned to cold water, not hot. I repeated that same mistake quite a few years after. 155 IQ.

CHAPTER 19

My first teaching post was to a small country school called Bourke. While I was there I learnt to play Rugby Union. I got very good at packing scrums. I would practice the drills and learn the moves, but I wasn't very good moving around the field.

I got worse the more tired I became. I couldn't read the play of the ball. I couldn't anticipate what the other team would do. There were numbers used for line-outs and I couldn't remember what they meant.

My team mates seemed to be understanding. When a line-out call was made, they'd remind me what to do. When the ref made a call, they'd explain it. They'd tell me where to go when a scrum was called.

I think the farmers, mechanics and other manual labourers thought it was funny they had to tell the degree holding Science teacher how to play a game.

I wanted to play well and would take advice from anyone who could help me. I did offer advice to one of my team mates though. I had trained with a rep team in order to try out for the Country team in the City verses Country competition and thought I'd learnt some things.

The person I picked to advise had actually played for Australia in the Under 21's side. Not the best choice. I took some pointers from him once I could get him to talk to me again.

I also learned to play tennis. Well, I actually learnt to hit a ball. Thankfully I played with people who were much better than me. Or they were thankful I played with them because I gave them a really big handicap.

Apparently tennis involves more than just hitting a ball. You are meant to be able to watch the other player and anticipate where the ball will come and move there in order to return the ball.

I learnt to hit the ball more often than miss it. The rest I couldn't do and I'd get worse through the night as I became more tired. I didn't get better as I warmed up.

I was always tired when I came home from school. I had flat-mates on occasion, but they were often out so I didn't have to work hard to understand what they were saying.

I enjoyed Rugby and Boxing training because it didn't involve emotional interpretation, just repetitive actions. New moves or techniques could be practiced over and over until I got them right.

CHAPTER 20

I enjoyed teaching for the most part, early on in my career. I liked Science because I got to blow things up and set things on fire. I was also allowed to cut up rats, brains, eyeballs, kidneys, hearts, lungs and intestines. I didn't understand why not everyone shared my enthusiasm for it.

Teaching became an obsession for me. I had no other distractions except the sports I did so I could focus a lot on teaching. Home was not a drain because I didn't have to worry about saying inappropriate things. I could sit where I wanted, eat what I wanted, read what I wanted and watch what I wanted. I didn't have to worry about breaking other people's rules. I enjoyed my life.

After four years at Bourke, in 1997, I moved to a coastal town and started teaching at a new school. I bought my own home and so life was still good.

It was harder at the new school because there were more teachers, and many more students, but because I lived on my own, I could have as much down time as I needed.

I know I frustrated my fellow teachers because I was very dis-organized. I believed I taught well, and I managed a class well, but I was terrible at the "behind the scenes" activities required of teachers.

Like other things, it wasn't that I didn't care or didn't try; I was simply very bad at it. I would regularly do eighty hour weeks, for months at a time trying to get the other things done because of how long it would take me.

There was a time when I taught a number of classes who sat state exams. This meant that when the exam period was over they could leave school earlier in the year than other classes.

This gave me more time off classes when they left. If other teachers were away that day I could be asked to fill in classes for them. If not, I used the time for what I wanted. I would get my work done and then read.

What I could have been doing though was helping my fellow Science teachers with their work. It didn't even cross my mind. I was not being deliberately selfish. I didn't see them doing their work and think, "I'm not going to help, I've done enough work of my own."

A person who had matured beyond their early ego-centrism would naturally see the need and step in to help. Their justifiable expectations were that I would do the same. But I didn't. I continued reading my books and relaxing in complete ignorance of my selfishness.

Eventually one of the teachers spoke to me about it. When he mentioned it I immediately saw what I should have done and started helping.

He was very hostile when he talked to me and I couldn't understand why. I didn't know why they just didn't tell me earlier and he didn't know why I would have to be told at all.

I taught at that school for five years. During that time I became more involved in the church I attended. During the year 1999 I developed a new obsession. Her name was Tania. We were married in April 2000. We had a son in October 2001.

CHAPTER 21

1999 to 2001 were difficult years for me in terms of teaching. While I split my attention between work and church and I still had my downtime at home I was ok. When I spent more time with Tania, it involved me focusing a lot of energy in trying to understand emotional communication and connection. I was confused about how I felt, because I didn't understand how I felt. I knew I was constantly tired, although I didn't know why.

Tania had two daughters from a previous marriage, and so when we were married I suddenly had a full house and I wasn't prepared for it. I was very happy; however, I found that I no longer had any downtime.

I would be emotionally drained from school by the time I got home, and rather than being able to have time on my own, I had a household of people I had to relate to.

At the end of 2000 I was placed under investigation for incompetence in teaching. A student had accused me of it and his father pressed the issue hard. I spent the Christmas holidays stressed over the whole thing.

I slept very little. I was afraid I would lose my job. I didn't know what was involved in the investigation. I felt I had done my best, but what if I hadn't? Or what if my best wasn't good enough?

The following year I found out that the complaint had been escalated and handed over to the State Education Department, rather than Local or Regional. It couldn't get any higher than this.

The whole school and primarily the Science faculty would be investigated as well. By the time the investigation was finished I had lost thirty kilograms in weight. My face was drawn and most of my muscle tone was gone.

Even though I was cleared of all accusations, I couldn't go back to school without feeling like I would vomit. By the end of 2001 I had to leave teaching. I just couldn't go back.

Even though I said that it was a change in career path, the truth was that although I didn't recognise it at the time, I had experienced a breakdown.

Common sense said to finish my tenth year teaching and take long service leave, but I just couldn't face walking back into the school again. The combination of the stress of the investigation and the emotional drain I experienced trying to adapt to a new family as well as that from teaching and church activity was too much for me.

CHAPTER 22

Over the next couple of years I tried and failed in a number of different business and work ventures. I even failed at concreting labouring.

I was asked by my boss one time to dig a few meter square holes that concrete could be poured into. It took me a very long time to get the measurements exact. Sometimes I had to put extra dirt in to fill up the hole.

Other times the hole would get too wide and I wasn't sure how to stick dirt back on the sides of the hole. There was a tree root in one of the holes that I just couldn't cut through with the shovel.

My mind was so fixated on trying to get those holes exactly one meter square that I didn't think about getting the axe from the back of the truck.

I started improving as my mind and body adjusted to doing things I had never done before; however, I still suffered high levels of anxiety and that blocked me from thinking through required actions.

I went into my "default mode" of thinking and I had trouble understanding even simple instructions. The boss may have had the neatest darn meter square holes on the planet, but he still had to let me go. He told me that my gifting lay in other areas.

Eventually I was able to get a job with a tutoring organization and I picked up casual teaching roles at a private school. More regular money came in and finally I got a position as a teacher at the private school where I had been casual teaching.

It was hard to go back into an environment that had hurt me so much before in the past. I had a constant expectation that I would be accused of incompetence in my teaching. I doubted my ability to communicate a message.

I never showed my doubts but I would forget to smile more and more. I went back to teaching, no matter what it cost me emotionally and physically, because it was the only thing I seemed able to do.

Money came into the house and we began to pay off our debts.

CHAPTER 23

I taught at the school for six years. Sometimes it was part time, sometimes full time. I was happy to teach part time because I found it difficult doing the work my wife and I did at the church as well as teaching full time. During this time Tania and I were running the children's ministry. We had a team of around seven adults and ten teenagers, with, at times, seventy to eighty children.

During 2008 and 2009 the school was placed under a great deal of pressure. The leadership of the school experienced the pressure and it could be felt by the other people who worked in the school.

General emails began to be sent around about people needing to do their jobs better. They would say that official warning letters would be sent out if things didn't improve. I began to feel more stressed because I didn't know if it was me. I would try harder and do more but the general emails would still come round.

In 2009 Tania and I were able to buy a house. We had sold our first house some time after I had resigned from teaching at the end of 2001. I had been working part time but I took on more work covering for a teacher who was sick. I was also given extra classes to look after when other teachers were away sick. This resulted in me regularly being on class twenty three lessons out of twenty five.

I also had playground duties and ran my own detentions as I believed in dealing with discipline problems myself rather than passing them on to others.

I was still leading the children's ministry with my wife, I was doing all the paperwork and marketing for my wife's business and organising meals and some housework as my wife worked late during the week and she did Saturday work as well.

By the middle of 2009 I'd had my second breakdown. This time it was a lot worse. I took everything Tania said the wrong way. I would shout at her. I went into clinical depression and had to battle thoughts of not wanting to go on.

I had extreme anxiety, panic attacks and found it difficult to drive. I couldn't go into shopping centres. When I tried to I would break out in a sweat and start shaking. I couldn't breathe properly and my heart would race. I couldn't force myself to move. I would have memory lapses and forget how to do some of the simplest of tasks.

I was prescribed anti-depressants and was required to see a psychologist and I did slowly improve. I was off teaching for nearly two months and then gradually worked my way back into it. I only worked part time again. I stepped out of children's ministry. I couldn't do any more than teach.

In 2010 my work load at school was cut down to half a day a week. I needed to find other employment in order to keep up the house payments. I applied for a job as a school chaplain but was rejected.

Not long after, the leadership team of our church was told of an opportunity to take on the pastoring of a church in another town. I believed God said to take the responsibility for it and so we became pastors of a church. That was when it got really bad.

PART 8 – CHRISTIANITY

CHAPTER 24

I grew up in a Christian home and I gave my life to Jesus when I was eight years old. I recognized early our need for a Savior, particularly my little sister's need. Either she was going to kill herself with her crazy behavior, or Mum and Dad were going to kill her out of frustration (I had heard Mum make comments about it).

The fact that neither of those things happened to her, I believe is testament to my first prayer as a believer, "Jesus," I said. "Please come into my sister's life. She really needs you."

I found out later that the whole salvation thing doesn't work that way, but I don't think the prayer hurt. At least my intentions were good. It would certainly have made my life easier if she was better behaved.

Unfortunately, my belief that my sister needed Jesus was based on my apparent lesser need for Him. For most of my Christian journey I held a core belief that I had to behave a certain way in order to be accepted by Jesus.

My salvation was based on my efforts. Of course Jesus did it all on the cross, but we have to do the rest. Grace was a cognitive concept of which I had no revelation.

I had a difficult time understanding forgiveness. It was hard for me to give it and it was just as hard for me to receive it. My idea of forgiveness was to push the incident aside until the impact of it disappeared. I can't say 'forgotten' as I rarely forgot any perceived slight. It was always stored away for later use.

The other problem I had was that I didn't like to be wrong. Being wrong meant some kind of failure on my part, a defect or inadequacy. It opened me up for rejection and ridicule and so I didn't like admitting fault of any kind.

I would verbally admit fault because I had found that to be quite an effective way of reducing the severity of punishments. Internally I would push the blame on to someone or something else and increase my right to be angry with them or it. This would then be added to my list of things to be remembered and brought up whenever I needed them.

CHAPTER 25

I believed that God spoke to me in my early teens and told me that I was going to be a pastor. While I was still in school, I looked at Bible College courses. I went to Bible study groups; I read commentaries and did everything in church I could to help out. I didn't do it because I was going to be a pastor, I did it because I found great satisfaction in it.

I enjoyed reading the Bible, I enjoyed prayer, and I loved doing things to help out in church, no matter what it was. It felt like I belonged there.

My parents discouraged my pursuit of becoming a pastor. They were Christians but they knew what a pastor's life was like and didn't want that for their son. Pastors were always poor. Dad encouraged me to pursue other career avenues.

In hindsight I can see the wisdom in his advice of having a qualification outside of a ministerial one. At the time it just seemed like Dad discouraging me from following my dreams.

I did what Dad said though because the Bible said that children should obey their parents, and Jesus wouldn't like me if I didn't.

My Christianity seemed to mostly involve me trying to lessen the severity of my sin, disguise it or justify it. If I couldn't do that, I would find ways to make my life a misery until I felt I had been appropriately punished. The sin was still there but at least it was paid for. Naturally I had to deal with a lot of shame and guilt as a result of that.

I still had a relationship with God. I read the Bible and had amazing prayer time where I encountered the supernatural power of God. I prayed for people and saw healings, including broken bones being mended. I saw visions, had words of knowledge for people, gave prophecies and cast out demons.

Those events though were limited to my belief about whether or not God could use me at that time based on my purity levels. I felt that God was more able to use me if it had been a longer period of time between sins and of course if the last sins were less severe, there was less time required.

CHAPTER 26

I had a good understanding about many things in the Christian life, but I had revelation about little. Much of what I had was head knowledge and I taught it quite well. I knew a lot of the Bible but most of it was letter not Spirit.

When I gave a message, it was good teaching but there was very little life in it. I would focus on presenting the words of the message and not the heart. For me, the focus was always what the words were, not the heart or Spirit behind the words.

This was a reflection of my understanding of conversation. If someone was relating an event and they weren't accurate I felt it was important to correct them. In most cases, I wasn't trying to embarrass them, I was trying to save them embarrassment by stopping them relating wrong information.

I reserved harsh judgement for pastors who willingly gave incorrect information from the pulpit. If they misquoted scripture, took it out of context or twisted it for their own purposes I would become very angry. In fact I would get angry if they used internet stories as part of their sermon to help illustrate a point and hadn't taken the time to check out if they were true or not.

I still get angry (perhaps indignant is a better word since I do want to do something about it) when I see a pastor twisting scripture in order to support the point they are trying to make. I am not so quick to judge pastors if I feel they are simply repeating what they've been taught. Of course, I think they should research to make sure what they've been taught is true.

This emphasis on words did lead to a number of conversational difficulties and often rejection. People don't really appreciate others correcting them.

I discovered that very few people shared my understanding that my corrections were for their betterment. I wasn't keen on people correcting me, but then their corrections were usually wrong and I would go to great lengths to prove it.

CHAPTER 27

I believe that my journey towards a better understanding of grace began around 1999. We had some guest singers, Jason and Glenda Hare, at our church and I remember having a God encounter where I received a revelation of Jesus who saved me and shed His blood for my forgiveness. The revelation wasn't complete, but it was a start.

It was not long after this that I remember having a conversation with my father and he got his words mixed around. I deliberately didn't correct him, saying to myself, "I don't have to, I know what he means."

I began to receive prayer ministry (from my friend and mentor, Daryll Goodsell) and a lot of it revolved around me receiving revelation of the Father's unconditional love for me. While there were many revelations during this time, there were three encounters that had powerful significance in my healing.

The first was where God changed my perspective of my earthly father. God the Father showed me that I viewed Him through the filter of my earthly father. He picked me up and shifted my position so that I viewed my earthly father through the filter of my Heavenly Father.

This meant that I began to see God the Father as He is shown to us through Jesus rather than being influenced by my experiences with my own father. It also meant that my encounters with my father could be reinterpreted as I saw him through the eyes of God.

In the second encounter I saw a picture of a glass vase. In it was a lump of coal-like black matter. I saw the hand of Jesus reach in and remove the lump from the vase. Jesus then told me that I was the vase and the lump was my sin.

He told me that He didn't just forgive my sin, but He removed it from my life. It was gone and it was forgotten. It was as if that sin had never been there in the first place.

I began to understand why I could boldly come into the throne room of grace. I started realising how grace gives us freedom from sin, rather than freedom to sin. My eyes were opening to the truth of the new creation and my heart was prepared for more revelation.

The third memorable encounter I had, involved a vision of a vulture. It was sitting on the branch of a dead tree. During the prayer the vulture flew away, but I knew it hadn't left permanently.

While this does not seem like much, it had great significance for me further down the path of my healing and deliverance.

A guest speaker, Mary Forsythe, ministered at our church. She gave a powerful testimony of the grace of God. She also helped me to be thankful for the things that had gone wrong in my life.

It was at her meetings that God showed me I was no different from Peter in my denial of Christ. I had not verbally denied my knowledge or relationship with Jesus. What I had done was to shrink back in fear and deny His power to overcome all obstacles to His plan being fulfilled.

I had expectations of certain things happening when I had started the business ventures I believed God had directed me to. Those expectations had not been met. The dreams I had with those businesses had died and I didn't believe that God had the power to fulfill dreams that had died.

Out of fear, pain and failure at the loss of my hopes and dreams I denied Jesus' ability and tried to do it on my own. Jesus poured love and acceptance over me and I repented of my denial.

I began to realise that God's love and acceptance for me was not based on what I had done, but on who He was. I began to weep as the pressure of performance was lifted off me. Joy and hope filled me as I released the future into His hands. The biggest sin I could think of was to deny Christ. I had done it and He still loved me.

I realised that if He loved me through that, then He would always love me. I didn't have to hide anything from Him. I didn't have to try to minimize or justify sin. I was free to accept I had done something wrong, repent of it (change my mind about wanting to do it), receive forgiveness and move on. Slowly but surely, I was changing from the inside out.

I am so glad that God did this foundational work before Tania and I took on the role of pastoring the church. The revelations I had received kept me going through the rough time we encountered as we began His work in the church.

PART 9 – MARRIAGE

CHAPTER 28

I was thirty years old when I got married. Most people saw that I was interested in Tania before I did. They used to say (not to my face), 'How dumb can you be and still breathe?'

My pastor asked me one time about how in touch with my emotions I was. I answered 'What emotions?' Of course I had emotions, I just didn't understand them or know how to express them. Emotions confused me, whether I experienced them or if they were directed at me from others.

I made a determination early on that I would not involve myself in relationships that would not head toward marriage. I didn't want to be hurt and I didn't want to hurt anyone else.

It makes it difficult to work out whether you'll marry a person if you don't know how you actually feel about them. It makes it doubly hard for you to approach a person if you can't tell what they think about you.

It was a miracle that Tania and I were married at all. I messed things up so often with inappropriate attitudes, comments and other misinterpretations that if it hadn't been God at work it would have finished before it started.

I am so thankful that I married Tania and no-one else because, apart from all the other good things about Tania, I don't think anyone else would have had the determination to make the marriage work and direct me to the right places to get the help I needed. Tania has truly kept our marriage vows of sticking with me through good times and bad, for richer or poorer, in sickness and in health.

CHAPTER 29

I started in the Children's Ministry at the church I was attending near the end of 1997. I wasn't long in there before Tania wanted me out. These were primary aged kids and I was used to teaching High School.

I didn't tolerate any breaching of the rules. The rules were there for everyone and if someone didn't appear to follow them, I would make sure they did. There would be no rule breakers in this man's Children's Church. I obviously didn't make a good first impression on Tania.

The leaders of the ministry didn't throw me out and I paid close attention to their expectations and adjusted my discipline methods over time. The leaders did a lot of skits and I enjoyed acting as a different person in them.

I also wrote plays. I thought they were funny. The kids seemed to like the one I wrote that had a scene where Santa nearly shot the Easter Bunny with a machine gun, but the adults in the main church didn't think it was appropriate!

As I spent more time at ministry meetings, lunches and actually doing the Sunday children's service I had more interaction with Tania. Something about her captivated my attention and whenever she spoke I made sure I didn't miss a word. Tania became one of the few people that I would have considered a good friend. That was what she was … a good friend.

Tania had two children and I didn't have any. I didn't know what kind of a dad I would be and I knew that if I married Tania I would take the two girls as my own daughters. In my mind that was the only option. Tania had done such an amazing job raising them and I didn't know if I could do it.

The other problem I had was that Tania was so far out of my league I didn't think I would have a chance and so I didn't want to get my hopes up. The best I could wish for was to be friends. So I was a friend.

I was a friend who got to church and stared at the door, tense until Tania arrived and only then relaxed. A friend (me) who drove with his eyes staring intently at every car in case it was Tania's (licence plate THX 168). A friend who would warn her about the dangerous advances of other men toward her. A friend who not only listened with complete focus as Tania shared her heart, but was able to share his heart with someone for the first time ever. Just a friend. IQ 155.

CHAPTER 30

When a couple of my cousins came to visit from New Zealand, I took them on a trip to a theme park. I asked my "friend" if she wanted to come. Tania agreed and the whole time there the only thing I wanted was to be close to her.

I wanted to go on every ride with her just in case I bumped into her. I wanted to walk next to her so I could brush her shoulder with mine. I wanted to touch her hand when she put it next to mine on the bench seat we were sitting on.

It was torture because she was just a friend and I knew that wanting to go further than friendship always resulted in rejection and pain. It was my experience and so it would happen again.

An image played in my mind of me touching Tania's hand and her pulling it away with a confused, angry look on her face. "What are you doing?" She would call out. "I trusted you," she would say. "You were my friend. Why would you do this?" she would ask. That would be the end. I would rather have her friendship than lose her for wanting more. My experience said it would be so.

So I did something stupid.

I didn't understand that Tania was starting to like me. The sharing and attention had made Tania feel special. She felt connected to me because I had opened my heart to her. She had begun to open her heart up to me. But I was afraid. I was afraid I would lose the best thing that had ever happened to me since I was eight years old and met Jesus.

I thought that if she thought I was pushing for more than friendship, then she would end what we had, so I told her that our time together wasn't a date. I told her I needed company for the drive as my cousins were staying in Sydney and we had to travel around three hours to get to our town in Port Stephens. I told her I appreciated her company, but not to think of it as anything more than that.

I thought I was doing the right thing, the thing that would put her at her ease. Fear and other confusing emotions bubbled around inside of me so I shut them down. I cut them off and when I talked to Tania, my words came out cold. They were distant and smacked of arrogance. Instead of protecting our relationship, I nearly destroyed it. And I didn't even know. I couldn't read Tania's signals at the theme park and I couldn't read her emotions after I had spoken to her.

We were at a prayer meeting not long after the trip and Tania was ignoring me. I didn't know what was wrong. I knew I felt horrible inside, but I didn't know what that feeling was. I was trying to pray but the only thing I did was question myself over what had gone wrong. Finally I felt God say, "You were arrogant."

"No I wasn't," I replied.

"You need to apologise," He said.

"What for?" I asked, genuinely confused.

"For being arrogant," He replied.

"I wasn't arrogant. I was trying to do the right thing by Tania," I argued.

I saw a picture of myself talking to Tania and I heard my tone of voice from a different perspective. It sounded arrogant. I hadn't meant it to but that was how it came out.

"You were arrogant," God said.

"I was arrogant," I agreed.

"You need to apologise," God said.

"I need to apologise," I agreed.

"Do it now!" God said.

I jumped and looked around. The meeting had finished and I couldn't see Tania anywhere. She must have already left. "Go out to the car park," flashed across my mind, the sense of urgency growing.

I started walking to the door to leave and someone stopped me to talk. I quickly finished up the conversation and continued out, but someone else started talking to me. Ministry matters. I excused myself as fast as I could and a third person moved to intercept me. Smile, nod, "nice to see you," side step and I'm out the door. It was too late. Tania had gone.

"Oh well," I thought, still not understanding the full implications of what had happened. "I'll catch up with her soon and do it then."

"No! Go home now and call." The urgency to apologise filled me and I got into the car.

As soon as I got home, I rang Tania. No answer.

"Call again!"

"What? I'll just wait a bit. She's probably not home yet."

"Call now!"

"Ok, I'll do it." I reached for the phone and my heart started pounding. I dialed the number and started sweating. My hands shook. I didn't understand what was happening. I was just calling to apologise to a friend I had hurt or offended.

Tania answered the phone. I apologise. It came from the heart. It wasn't a carefully planned script that I recited. The words came out before I could think about them or stop them, and that was rare for me.

Almost everything I said was scripted in some way. I designed my words to cause the least amount of offense possible. I almost always think through what words I will use and am careful about how they are presented.

My apology was accepted, and eventually forgiveness given. What I didn't realise was that if I hadn't called Tania and apologised that day, her heart would have been closed to me forever.

I found out later that Tania had felt I had been playing with her emotions. She could feel the emotions going through me, but my interest in her, followed by sudden arrogant lack of interest over and over again were gradually shutting off her feelings toward me.

CHAPTER 31

I didn't realise I was in love with Tania. I didn't know what love felt like. I couldn't understand the feelings associated with being in love.

While I was at Uni I had spoken to one of our tutors/lecturers. He was talking about his wife and so I asked him how he knew she was the one. This made him feel uncomfortable as it was an inappropriate question to be asking University lecturers and I was already in my early twenties.

I didn't pick up his discomfort or the inappropriateness of the conversation until quite a bit later. He answered me anyway and said that when they're the one, you'll just know.

I figured I'd know because they'd actually like me back. I wasn't the most positive person when it came to love. The point was, I didn't know. There was no 'just knowing.' Thankfully God knows what He's doing.

I was walking through a hall at the school I was teaching in at the time, singing one of the songs we sang at church; very quietly. I felt a warmth wash over me and peace and happiness flow through me.

It was a feeling I associated with God's presence and love. His love for me and my love for Him. Then Tania's face came into my mind. I immediately rebuked the spirit that would try to interfere with my time with God.

I began to sing again and those feelings stayed with me and Tania's face returned. I commanded that ungodly spirit of lust to get off me and to torment me no more and then returned to singing. That feeling remained with me and Tania's face stayed there.

It finally fell into place. God showed me how I experienced love with Him and then showed me that this is how I felt about Tania. He pointed out to me that I was in love with Tania. This wasn't me just liking Tania as a friend.

CHAPTER 32

I had been dreaming about Tania for some time. The dreams would usually involve Tania, her girls and I involved in family activities. In my teens I would often dream of a particular person too. The dream would involve a girl I didn't remember meeting before. She was usually trapped in a castle and I would rescue her.

When I thought back I realised it had been Tania in my dreams. It was only after we were married and we were talking about events in our lives that we realised we had crossed paths before when I was around fifteen years old.

A vision I had once of Tania and myself showed us as two big coal trucks. They travelled along parallel paths for a while and then they swerved in towards each other. They hit each other but instead of crashing, they merged into one much larger truck that could do more than either of them could on their own. I wasn't very good at picking up God's subtle hints.

After the sudden, unexpected and out of the blue revelation that I loved Tania as more than just a friend, God and I had a serious talk. It was Saturday morning 18th December 1999. I told God that I was thirty years old and I wanted to get married.

I said that I realised now that I was in love with Tania but that if I couldn't marry her, then I wanted these feelings gone because she was consuming my every thought.

I knew that she was way out of my league and I really didn't stand a chance, but I did want to be married and there was no-one else I wanted to be married to more. Plus I didn't know if I would be a good dad to her two daughters. "God!" I called out to Him. "What do I do? What do You want me to do?"

I felt Him reply, "What does My Word say about the desires of your heart?"

"If I delight in You, You will give me the desires of my heart," I replied.

"Do you delight in Me?" He asked. "Do you trust Me? Have you committed your ways to Me?" He continued.

"Yes," I answered. "Of course."

"Then what do you desire?" He asked me.

I nearly said that I desired a wife, but I paused and thought. I didn't just want a wife. I wanted a particular person to be my wife. I wanted Tania.

"Then what do you desire?" He asked me.

"I desire Tania," I replied.

"Done," I heard. Then I felt something hit my forehead and I was knocked back a step. The impression I received was of a seal being stamped on my head; a seal of approval. With that final slap to the forehead I finally understood what I was meant to do.

I went to see Tania to tell her about my feelings for her. I was shaking when I talked to Tania and she didn't make it any easier for me, but we officially started our relationship that day. We both believed that God had called us together.

Tania and I did go on a proper date. We went out to tea and chatted. I knew Tania had been married but I really didn't know much about her life before she became a new creation.

In truth it was none of my business. That person was gone and the Tania who sat before me was not the same Tania who existed before being born again. However, during the conversation over dinner I found an appropriate moment and asked her how many guys she had been with.

I also asked her if she'd been tested for AIDS or other sexually transmitted diseases. Yeah, I know. 155 IQ. It still surprises me.

Tania is so forgiving.

Tania and I were engaged on the 5th of January 2000 and we were married on the 15th of April that same year. It was one of the happiest days of my life. By the time we got back to my house, now our house, my face ached from the smiling. My muscles had been out of practice.

Going back to our house was not lack of planning or dumb smart person reasoning. We wanted our first night together to be in our home, in our bed. I had a stretched limo coming the next morning to whisk us away to the airport for our trip to Cairns.

CHAPTER 33

Our honeymoon had … difficulties. There were some great, fun times and tours. There was some confusion on one tour though when the tour guide asked for our name.

I told him our last name and he told me he wasn't asking me for the name of the town, he was asking for our last name. I told him our last name again and he sighed, slowed down his voice, spoke a little louder and said very patiently, one more time that he wanted to know our last name. Cairns is the name of the town, and he needed to know our last name.

I of course assumed that his ongoing questioning was because our name wasn't on the list and I started to panic. He seemed quite surprised when I spoke, not just in English but with an Australian accent.

I told him our last name was Cairns and that the travel agent had booked everything so our name should be there. He looked at the list, found our name, made a comment about that not happening very often and had a little laugh. I began to see the funny side of it too, eventually.

All people with Asperger's have hypersensitivity in areas. Bright lights are painful, loud noises and touch can hurt. Smells are offensive and certain tastes and textures can make them vomit.

I generally enjoy eating, but my favourite meats have always been devon and sausage. Apparently it has a lot to do with the texture and the lack of chewing required. My worst eating experience came in the form of ox tongue.

My mother wanted to try some new food. Trying new food is not an idea that will be met with encouragement in a family of people with Asperger's.

She boiled up the ox tongue but didn't peel the taste buds off so when I ate it, the taste buds rasped against my own tongue. I didn't eat any more than that first mouthful and haven't eaten any more since. I don't remember the taste, I only remember the feel.

It is because of this hypersensitivity that many men with Asperger's find certain honeymoon and marriage activities lacking in appeal. They will often have to go through a process of de-sensitization before the experience becomes as enjoyable for them as it is meant to be.

Men who are affected this way may not understand why they are not enjoying it and will find ways to blame their partner for their lack of enjoyment or ability to perform. I'm not sure if this specific aspect was a problem for me. It could have been, but I had enough other issues causing anxiety that I could blame Tania for.

Over many conversations with Tania, I had expressed some of my fears and insecurities, my sense of inadequacy and rejection as well as a generally low self-esteem. Tania had tried to allay my fears and told me a number of things about her last relationship.

Everything she said was placed in an incredibly positive context that said, "I love you. You are the one God has destined me for. I know that you will absolutely satisfy me in every possible way in this marriage. You are perfect for me and you are who I have been waiting my whole life to meet."

What I did instead was take pieces of each of those conversations and put them together in a way that I was certain was the truth, just like I was with Cindy the dog. The message I received was, "My well-endowed ex-husband had enough experience before I met him to give him a reputation that he was proud of and others spoke about with awe. He was physically fit and had a body that you shouldn't try to compare yourself to. You are not that good looking but God did tell me I had to marry you."

A thirty year old virgin man with inadequacy issues and Asperger's is not going to have a great honeymoon while obsessing over thoughts like that. Unfortunately, neither does his bride.

Of course there were some pleasant times as well. We sailed on a barrier reef cruise and then went underwater in a mini-sub. We visited the Daintree rainforest and travelled in a cable car up a mountain.

We also went white water rafting, although that was slightly marred by the fact that I had ripped off one of Tania's nails playing snap … with cards. Well, the winner was going to get a prize and both of us were keen to win.

We did have trouble convincing the emergency ward staff that the bride of a honeymooning couple had her fingernail ripped off during a card game. It was true though.

Tania had worn false nails for the wedding and they had been glued on hard. We both went for a snap, somehow Tania's nail clipped my hand and the nail, false and real one came off.

Well, it was almost off. The rest had to be taken off at the emergency ward. Tania was obviously not well, but I had bought a video of the wedding with me and some Maison. I thought I might be able to pull the night out from total disaster.

I lit some candles, poured the drinks and put the videos in the VCR. We found that the person we had asked to video the ceremony had taken more footage of his new wife than of the wedding. The sound was terrible quality and the battery had gone flat a number of times and he had missed large segments of the ceremony.

The drink was the wrong type and we didn't like the flavour. I became angry at everything going wrong, especially at Tania for telling me it was my fault her finger nail was ripped off. That meant that I had hurt her and Jesus wouldn't like me if I hurt someone. Naturally I tried to tell her it was not my fault. Her hand hit me and if she hadn't been so competitive it wouldn't have happened.

Apparently it was a teasing way to turn the situation into a bit of fun. If I apologised for it, cuddled her and tried to kiss her better the rest of the night might have been different. As it was, I nearly started a fight, but Tania said she was tired and sore and wanted to sleep. I told her that was a good idea and blew the candles out.

I blew the candles out with more vigour than I should have, and straight down on top of them. The result was that I caused hot wax to splash up over my face and chest. The weather was warm so I wasn't wearing a shirt. I decided that I didn't care how badly burnt I was, I was not going back to the emergency ward. That was how our marriage started.

CHAPTER 33

At the beginning I would bring flowers regularly. I would write letters and Tania was the centre of my attention. Within two years, our son was born, I had burnout and resigned from my secure teaching job.

At four years we had lost our house and our money. I had done six months of a law degree but had to pull out of it. I was passing it, but there was enough strain on the relationship without that too.

Tania had been able to fulfil one of her dreams of becoming a beauty therapist, but there wasn't enough money coming from it to cover our bills. I had attempted a number of businesses and failed with them.

Tania's and my relationship was breaking apart. I took everything Tania said the wrong way and we would fight all the time. Apart from fighting there was very little communication between us. I had closed myself off from Tania and I had become addicted to internet pornography.

I had never been involved in porn before then and I don't know why it got me after I was married. I was addicted to porn for about six months. It was only when I couldn't get out of it on my own or even with help from other men that I talked to Tania about it.

I received counseling for it and even talked to our senior pastor, telling him I was willing to step out of ministry until I was free of it. My confession about looking at porn was nearly the final straw of our relationship.

Tania had been able to put up with most of my inappropriate behaviour and comments but this was something else. Porn has a powerful negative impact on a person's mental, emotional and spiritual state.

To Tania, and most women, it was betrayal and no different to adultery. I might not have committed the physical act but I had been unfaithful with my heart, mind and eyes.

For a woman there is very little difference, except for the fact that most men attempt to downplay the effects of watching porn and so don't understand the ongoing emotional damage this betrayal does to their wives when they repeat the act over and over.

CHAPTER 34

By the time six years had passed, we were back on our feet again. I was working and had been freed from porn. We were involved in children's ministry in the church and Tania had her own beauty business going.

We were paying off our debts and getting out of the hole I dumped us in. I was learning new scripts and had begun to cope with the change in life that we experienced. I was receiving regular prayer ministry, trying to deal with issues I had begun to see in myself.

One major problem was that I had stopped romancing Tania. My interactions with her became mechanical. I based my current behaviours with her on past behaviours that had worked before.

I was very ritualistic and actions came from my head, not my heart. I had no passion, no joy and I certainly wasn't up for trying new things. While our marriage had improved, and we even had some good days together, it was still not good.

A person with Asperger's believes everyone thinks the same way they do. It came as quite a surprise to me when my psychologist told me that I would have to talk to Tania about things I thought were obvious.

If Tania had a morning off and I was working then surely it was obvious that she should get up and get Caleb ready for school so I could focus on getting myself ready. I would get up and get Caleb ready if she had to go to work.

I didn't understand why she didn't get up and help. Tania must see it needed doing, because I saw it did. In my mind that meant Tania was either lazy or didn't care about me. I harboured a lot of resentment over that.

I couldn't comprehend that Tania wouldn't see it because she didn't think the same way I did.

This repetitive behaviour and belief that Tania thought like me led to many disputes.

If you ask any lady if they like receiving flowers, more often than not they will say yes. This is not true.

The truth is, she likes receiving flowers as long as she is not receiving them regularly. Buying flowers each week is great, for the first couple of weeks. After that it gets boring. It gets repetitive.

"Do you like the flowers Tania?" I ask excitedly while handing her a bunch of flowers for the eighth week in a row.

"Yeeessss," She replies carefully.

I've heard that yes before. It means "not really"'

"You don't like the flowers?" I ask.

"No, I do. It's just that … umm. Well it's summer and it's getting hot and I don't like watching the flowers die."

"But it was summer and hot four weeks ago and you seemed to like the flowers then?"

"Yes, but it's just that I've had flowers now a few weeks in a row and it would be nice to get something different."

"But you said you like flowers."

"I do like flowers."

"If you like flowers, how come you don't like these? They're your favourite colours. I always buy you these colours because you like them."

"I do like these flowers. They're beautiful."

"If you like them, how come you don't want them? How come you want something different? If I like something, I don't want anything else."

"Yes, but surely you get bored with things, even if you like them?"

"No. If I like them, I like them. Why would I get bored if I like them? If I got bored with them, it would mean I didn't like them."

"Give me an example."

"I like devon sandwiches."

"But you must get bored with eating them."

"No. I've eaten them nearly every school day my entire school life. In fact sometimes I would even get to have them on the weekends when I toasted them."

"Well sometimes I can still like something but not want it. Sometimes I can like something but want something else."

"I don't get it."

"You don't have to get it. Just understand that that's the way I am. Just because I say I like something, doesn't mean that I want that all the time. I like different things too. And just because I really liked what you did yesterday, doesn't mean I'm going to like the same thing today."

"Well, how will I know what you're going to like and what you won't like?"

"I'll always like it. I'll just want you to do something different so you'll just have to try something and find out."

"But … but … umm."

"Just get in touch with my emotions and feel what I would like."

Tania smiles at me like that's the answer to all the problems. I start to shake because that answer was the cause of my problems.

CHAPTER 35

As you can imagine, this mentality of mine carried over into all aspects of married life, including the bedroom. I liked routine. I did everything the same way. What worked before would be used over and over again. If Tania tried to speak to me about it, I would take offense and feel that she was attacking my manhood. I would roll over and sulk or start arguing with her and tell her why it was all her fault.

I would try to follow the "10 Steps to Happiness," and while that was OK for a while, ten years of the "Ten Steps" does not really lend itself to developing intimacy. My genuine desire was to make Tania happy; however, my repetitive behaviour made Tania feel like I was treating her like a machine. "If I push these buttons in this order then I will get this result."

Asperger's excluded humanity and emotion, and love making became an act, not an intimate moment where two humans connected with each other physically, mentally, emotionally and spiritually.

I needed to connect with Tania emotionally, to feel what she wanted me to do. If I couldn't do that, then at least be creative, to try different things and more importantly, to release the desire and passion I had for her and allow her to feel that. But it was only on rare occasions that happened. I didn't want things to be that way, but I didn't know how to change.

CHAPTER 36

Over the next few years, things did improve. Tania and I grew closer, we worked better as a team than we had before. We had greater revelation of God's love and grace and I came out of my cave. This was the result of prayer ministry as well as me adapting to new situations and learning more effective scripts.

Our relationship was on the mend and Tania was opening up to me once more. We bought a house at a beautiful place called Fingal Bay in New South Wales, Australia. It was five minutes' walk from the beach, had three bedrooms, the master with a full ensuite, a double garage, a spa bath, a third toilet and a pool. It was less than seven years old and we bought it for $20,000 less than the original buyer paid for it when he bought it off the plan. It was an incredible blessing.

We purchased the house at an auction. We had a loan pre-approved from a bank. I was going to look at the auction just to see what they were like. I called the real estate agent and told him I wasn't going to be entering the auction.

For some reason I told him how much our loan was approved for. He held up the auction for me,

and then held it up longer until Tania got there with a cheque book.

When the auction started, I opened the bidding with the total amount our loan was approved for and the other person in the auction said nothing.

Tania and I became the proud owners of a house that I had done no inspections for or even compared possible prices of. I felt sick. I shook, turned white and nearly passed out.

I had broken every rule there was in house buying, especially for auctions. I hated breaking rules.

What I found out later was that the reserve price was exactly the amount I had bid. If I had bid lower, we would have missed out on the house.

There was nothing wrong with the house and we became the talk of the real estate agents in the area. I had seen a few and told them what I was looking for and around how much I was willing to pay and been told that it would never happen in the area we lived.

I was a nervous wreck for quite some time after though, just waiting for something to go wrong. I had broken the rules for house buying and I just knew something was going to bite us. Nothing ever did. And just over a year later we left it behind.

CHAPTER 37

Tania and I believed we had heard the call of God to take responsibility for a church in a small town. We were led to believe certain things about the church that weren't quite true. We were told that there were around forty attendees. There were about twenty. We were told that the pastors had been on a bit of an income. The pastors had been on an income but the church bills hadn't been paid.

There were debts totaling nearly $30,000. I entered a new job, having to learn new skills, while at the same time trying to pick up casual teaching work. I am so thankful for the church we came out of for managing the administrative side of the church for the first two years. Tania and I would not have survived it if they hadn't.

The beginning of 2012 saw us taking responsibility for the administration side of the church too. This was more stress for me, more learning and less sleep.

I had gone into default mode not long after taking the church. It was a time when Tania and I should be pushing closer together, but instead, I withdrew inside myself, trying to cope with the new situations.

It would have been great to be able to lean on each other and grow through the circumstance, but I didn't do it. In fact my emotional withdrawal left Tania feeling alone in a place where she didn't know anyone or have any support.

I again started taking everything Tania said the wrong way. I made cases against her using events that occurred ten years and more ago. I was suspicious of her motives and unable to see everything that she was doing to make life easier for me.

I would say that the nearly four years as pastors, until my healing, were the worst years of an already difficult marriage for Tania.

We received very little in terms of wages from the church and I was no longer able to teach and work on running the church. We ran into financial difficulties and had to sell our house again. We were unable to pay the strata fees on it as well as pay the mortgage. While I was teaching we injected a lot of money into the church to help pay off the debts.

As pastors, we were required to attend the state and national conferences for our movement. These were terrible for Tania. I wouldn't last a day of lights, noise, movement and social interaction and I would start to have melt downs. I would need to go to our apartment at every break and shut myself in a dark room with no sound and try to rest.

When the music was on I would leave the auditorium or whatever room it was played in. I would argue with everything Tania would say. I would be offended, insulted and upset with Tania, not just over small things, but over nothing. My mind would hear things she didn't say, and put it in a way she never would have meant.

My reactions to Tania became louder and more aggressive. While I never swore at Tania or touched her aggressively, the tone used, my body posture and the accusations made were all abusive. I constantly felt like I was being attacked (even though I never was) and I aggressively defended myself.

Our relationship was not good at all. After I made it past the aggression I would apologise and then the depression would work on me. I realised that I was messing up Tania's life and my son's. In order for her to be truly fulfilled, she needed to have someone else. Someone who could look after her properly, to connect with her emotionally, provide for her effectively and be intimate with her the way a man and wife should be. Our relationship had the depth and intimacy of flatmates.

At times, Tania would ask me to be more romantic. To bring flowers, to do something to show her that I was thinking of her. I didn't change. In fact I would usually argue with her. I'd tell her I was doing my best and that she should stop nagging me, even though she may have only mentioned it once over the last three months.

I would usually find some argument as to why she just didn't see what I did for her. I'm pretty sure that one time I told her that she didn't like the flowers last time I got them, possibly three years before.

I would usually try to turn the request around to tell Tania that it was all her fault. If she persisted, I would become aggressive or I would sulk again.

I would immerse myself in my work so I wouldn't have to have those kinds of conversations and this of course made the problem worse. The worse it got, the more Tania tried to tell me how she was feeling. The more she told me, the worse I felt about my ability to be a good husband. The worse I felt the more distant I became. The more distant I was the more persistent and insistent Tania became.

Tania wasn't asking for much. She really just wanted me to show her she was a part of my life; to let her know she was important to me. I took it the wrong way and felt that she was telling me I was a bad husband. And I didn't do anything about it.

Unfortunately our arguments were the only place that Tania could get any emotional connection with me or any real attention from me for that matter. I saw the pattern that formed and began to recognise the baiting Tania would use to start a fight.

Instead of changing and dealing with it, I started ignoring the baiting as well. It amazes me that

Tania stayed and fought for our marriage like she did.

CHAPTER 38

Another issue that was discovered was a problem with my pituitary gland. I had damaged it playing rugby and as a result it stopped producing the chemical needed to stimulate the production of testosterone. This increased my sense of having an inability to be the man that Tania needed. I believed she would be better off without me.

Tania had been asking me to look at life insurance and so I took it out. It was part of a carefully laid plan where I could leave Tania with a nice package of money and free her to be with someone better than I was.

I honestly believed that this action was honourable and would be better for both Tania and Caleb in the long run. These are not normal thoughts.

During this time we ran a church, counseled couples and ministered to others. We organised guest speakers and the church continued to grow. A youth group was started, the children's ministry was kicked off, we found people to help with worship, and even found some musicians. An op-shop was opened and the kiosk and charitable food program the church ran before we arrived continued.

There were other activities that the church ran as well in order to assist the community. It just goes to show that God can use anyone to accomplish His plan. God doesn't call the qualified, He qualifies the called.

During this time, Tania had many battles of her own. One of them was coming to terms with the fact that she would never have the emotional connection she wanted in her relationship.

We were told there was no cure for Asperger's and that we would have to learn management strategies to lessen the arguments and to help us understand each other.

What Tania had noticed though, was that there were times we had connected emotionally. There were times we had gotten along with each other and understood one another.

Tania believed that God gives us the desires of our heart and her desire was for us (not her and some other man) to experience connection at a very deep level. Tania didn't believe that this was a situation that we had to put up with and make the most of. She believed that there was a way to beat this problem, not just manage it.

We organised to see a doctor to sort out the libido problem. I received regular prayer ministry. We began to see some breakthrough, even though I would revert to default mode.

I remember trying to get ready to go to church one time and Tania was talking to me. I knew I was going to have to leave soon and I was being held up. I became frustrated and yet at the same time I was enjoying Tania's company. I wanted to go but I wanted to stay and kiss her. I was frustrated with her but I loved her deeply.

I had never experienced two emotions at the same time before. It had always been one or the other. I would either experience love or frustration, not both of them together. Things were changing and I started fighting too.

PART 10 - HEALING AND DELIVERANCE

CHAPTER 39

While I received some freedom gradually, some came instantaneously. It was during some Sozo ministry (please look at http://bethelsozo.com/ for more information) that I received incredible breakthrough. At this point, if you haven't read the Introduction, please do it now.

The following is not a formula, it is simply a description of what happened for me. The links that I saw between certain spiritual influences, religions and symptoms of Asperger's may in fact be unique to me.

If you are looking for freedom from Asperger's, then you will need to seek God to let Him show you what needs to happen in your life.

It was Friday night after youth and I was having an adult meltdown. I was bad tempered and full of accusations. Tania tried to help me see the truth but I knew what was right and nobody could tell me I was wrong.

I knew that Tania had been taking someone else's side against me; again, and I could and did list all the times she had done it, and I wasn't going to have it. Things had to change.

After everyone had gone I let loose. I thought I was reasonable and right and it made me mad when Tania tried to tell me I was wrong.

Eventually Tania told me that if I was behaving like this now, there was no way she was going to conference with me when there would be so much more pressure.

I lost it and stormed out of the building, slamming doors and revving the car engine. I sped off, although not too fast because I didn't want to break the law and get a speeding ticket.

I parked in a supermarket parking lot to try to calm down. I didn't know how long I would stay away from home.

It would serve Tania right if I didn't come back after the way she treated me. Perhaps this was it. Perhaps this was the end of the relationship. Maybe our marriage was finally over and after all I had done to make it work too.

I finally did return home after a number of hours. Caleb was still awake. At least he was worried about me, not like Tania. She didn't care. I glared at her. I started to talk at her but she held up her hand.

"I don't want to talk to you when you're like this," she said.

I hated it when she did that. I didn't say any more to her but I sure showed her. I grabbed my pillow out of our bedroom and went to sleep in the spare room. That'll teach her.

I woke the next morning determined to give Tania another chance to redeem herself. I lay in bed for a bit longer and tried to relax.

I calmed down and I realised that I wasn't right. I didn't want to be apart from Tania. I didn't want to be acting this way. When I heard Tania get up in the morning I went to apologise and said that I needed some prayer with her.

CHAPTER 40

I had previously made a list of things I do when I get into fights with Tania. They were defence mechanisms that I employed to get my own way. We began to go through the list, forgiving people from my past generations and then asking Jesus to deal with whatever needed dealing with.

This is one tiny part of what happens in Sozo ministry. I am not trying to explain Sozo or describe how it is done. See the website above for more information if you want it or to find someone who can minister to you using it.

I am not a trained Sozo minister and so don't use what I write as techniques for Sozo ministry. There are differences in every Sozo ministry session as it relies on guidance from the Holy Spirit as He ministers to each individual in the way they need.

After this I saw a picture of myself with a vulture holding a knife. If you are reading this and you have Asperger's you are probably saying that the vulture is a bird and birds don't have hands. How can a bird hold a knife? Well, this was a vision. A vision can give the impression of what is happening in the spiritual realm.

Perhaps a more accurate description would be to say that I saw what I believed to be a spirit that looked a lot like a vulture holding a knife.

The vulture/spirit repetitively stabbed me all over my body with the knife. Tania and I thought about possible meanings of it. I remembered the encounter I had with a vulture in a previous time of prayer ministry. I thought perhaps it could be a spirit of death but we waited for God's instructions before doing anything.

I then saw the vulture stab the knife through the top of my head and into my brain. That was when I realised that the vulture was associated with Asperger's. I linked the stabbing all over the body to the hypersensitivity associated with Asperger's.

Jesus then walked into the scene and the vulture fled. Jesus walked over to me, hugged me and began to heal the wounds. As He did so He said, with what I felt was a certain sense of pride, "Look at you. You're still standing. What strength!"

To clarify, this did not leave me feeling like I was better than anyone else. Jesus was not comparing me to anyone and He was not saying that I was more suitable for ministry than other people because I had remained standing in spite of the opposition.

These were words of truth I needed to hear in order to bring healing into the wounds of my heart. They were really along the lines of "Well done, good and faithful servant," but they were said exactly the way I needed to hear them.

They were words that overcame my sense of inadequacy, the feelings of being less than a real man and the belief that I was a disappointment to Jesus because of my constant failings.

The scene changed again and this time I saw a long line of men, with me standing at one end of the line. I looked to the other end and standing above the line was the vulture. It felt like it had set itself up as some kind of god that ruled over my generational lines. The line of men represented the generations of my family.

I forgave down the generational lines and broke the ties to it. I then came out of agreement with Asperger's. As I watched, I saw Jesus step up to the vulture, grab it by the neck, snap the neck and then throw the vulture away.

I have never seen Jesus be violent in a vision before and it surprised me. I know that Jesus overturned the money changer's tables and whipped them. I know that Jesus didn't hold back in addressing the behaviour of Pharisees.

I also know that descriptions of God's behaviour when He acted out of righteous anger in the Old Testament were violent. I was just surprised with the anger that Jesus had toward this spirit.

CHAPTER 41

Jesus then stood in the position the vulture had held and He called forth the generational blessings. He spoke restoration of the blessings over the generational line.

Our family line seems to be connected to druidism. The impression I received was that druids were blessed with sensitivity to the spirit realm and an ability to operate powerfully in it. This was originally given as a gift to help others encounter the presence of God. Instead it was perverted and used by the enemy in an attempt to pull people away from God, and replace Him with a false light.

I believe that the restoration of the generational blessing brought back the purity of the gift and will allow it to be used to bring glory to God. I know that I have always hungered for the supernatural and in the past had looked for it in science fiction and fantasy books. For me they held an addictive quality, particularly the stories involving magic and sorcery.

These are counterfeits and I believe that God wanted to give me, as He wants to give everyone, real, pure, Godly, supernatural encounters. In truth, according to Kathie Walters, we have them all the time. We just need to get our antennas operating and our hearts receptive to the fact that Godly supernatural encounters are meant to be a normal part of the Christian life.

After Jesus had called out the restoration of the generational blessing, He came to stand next to me. He looked at me and told me that He had wanted to do this for a long time. He had waited for one member of the generations to say yes to Him. Then He said, "And it was you." I realised then the difference between the "called" and the "chosen." The chosen have simply said "yes."

I was not better or more gifted than any of my ancestors. I didn't have a better heart and I wasn't more qualified. I wasn't more righteous, worthy or deserving than anyone else. The invitation to open the door for God to set the generational line free had been given to every one of my ancestors. All of them were called just like I was. My only part was to accept the invitation.

His love for me was not changed by the decision I made to say yes. His love for me, as it is for the entire population of the world, is not based on my character or behaviour, but on His. He is love and so He loves completely and unconditionally.

Jesus' capacity to bring salvation, healing and deliverance to my family line didn't depend on my ability. In fact it was the Holy Spirit who bought me to a place where I recognised my complete inability to change myself and that allowed me to say "yes" to the invitation.

One hundred percent of the salvation, healing and deliverance of my family line was accomplished by Jesus Christ when He finished His work on the cross. I was simply led to the place where that truth became real in my life, and I accepted it on behalf of my family. It is ALL about Him.

The only distinction between the called and the chosen, before, during or after an encounter with Christ, is the word "yes." I also believe that it is God Himself that brings us to a place where we say yes anyway. None of it is us, not even 0.5%. It is all, one hundred percent Him.

Out of interest I wanted to see where the symbolism of the vulture was used so the next day I performed a Google search on vulture emblems.

One of the sites said that Tutankhamen had a headpiece with a vulture next to a snake on it. It was apparently common for the pharaohs to have these on their headpieces. The vulture was a symbol that represented a goddess of protection.

I found this interesting as my wife and I had both noticed that the symptoms of Asperger's intensified when I was under greater levels of stress or if I felt I was being attacked.

The snake (a cobra or asp) represented the pharaoh's divinity. I found this interesting too, considering the ego-centricity of people with Asperger's.

I knew that both sides of my family had strong connections with Freemasonry and/or Druidism. It seems that there are ties between both Druidism and Freemasonry and ancient Egyptian religious beliefs.

While I am not sure of the accuracy of this, I do know that in the ministry sessions I received, God did link Asperger's, Druidism and Freemasonry with the vulture and I had no idea about the symbols on the pharaoh's headpieces. Kathie Walters explains that Druidism and Freemasonry are both rooted in the same Egyptian Spirits. Osirus and the All seeing eye. There are others too.

Does this mean that if you have Asperger's you must have links with Druidism and Freemasonry? Could it mean that Druidism and Freemasonry cause Asperger's? The answer is I am not sure but it certainly seems to be an influence

If you are receiving ministry for Asperger's, let the Holy Spirit show you what He wants to do in you. These are links He made with me and they may be unique to me. One thing for sure is that The Holy Spirit is the revealer of hidden things.

CHAPTER 42

Something that was also important was that we prayed for physical healing as well. We prayed for growth in the area of my brain that been stunted as a result of Asperger's.

We also prayed for God to burn new pathways of thinking and to remove the old ones. We prayed the nerves in my brain that hadn't functioned normally would fire up properly and the ones that were dormant would have new life breathed into them.

Not long after this, Tania had a vision of bats flying all around me. We looked at a book called "The Divinity Code," by Adam Thompson and Adrian Beale. They said, among other things that in a dream or vision, bats can represent a blind spirit associated with the occult.

This interpretation grabbed my attention as I felt God speak to me that it was related to the lack of a conscience I experienced (a trait common to people with Asperger's). What I knew as right or wrong came only from what I read in the Bible or from having been punished in the past.

There was no innate sense of right or wrong in me. There was no inner voice to tell me not to do anything. If I didn't do something then what stopped me was usually the thought of punishment.

My decisions for behaviours were usually based on what punishment I might receive if I got caught, not on the morality of it. When we prayed, I felt God was freeing me from a blinding of my conscience and of inappropriate words or behaviours.

CHAPTER 43

Later on we had some ministry at church about moving to new places in God. It was about being caught up in fear of the future and not moving into the destiny God has for us. The preacher mentioned that unforgiveness can hold us back in the past.

While I had made an attempt to forgive, there was something inside of me that had never let go of offences. True forgiveness involves releasing the person who sinned against you from that action. It means that the action never needs to be bought up again because Jesus is looking after it.

I would regularly bring up offences from other people, usually Tania, and build a case against them. I had moved ahead in many areas of my life and tried many new things, but emotionally I hadn't grown and I knew that my relationship with Tania wouldn't develop if I didn't truly forgive her.

There was something around me that showed itself like a lawyer, an accuser. If something went wrong in our relationship and Tania tried to talk to me about it I would bring up things that had happened even before we were married to tell her why the issue was all her fault. I had to build a case against her. And maybe some of those things had actually happened, but the only reason they were having an effect on me now was because I hadn't let them go.

So even if I was right about the events, I was still wrong in so many other ways that actually counted. I needed to deal with unforgiveness. I wanted to move on.

I saw a picture of an old house and I was standing on its veranda. On the street I saw a white limousine with its back door open. I walked down the steps of the veranda toward the limousine and my father came out of the house.

"Where are you going?" my father asked.

"I can't stay here anymore. I have to leave." I replied.

"But if you leave, you'll get hurt. You'll fail and you won't be able to defend yourself. Don't you see? You have to stay here. It's the only way you'll be safe. You're not going to make it out there. You don't have what it takes. How many times have you failed in the past? I love you and I'm just trying to help. I warned you before about trying new things and see where it got you? I just want to protect you"' my father said.

"Dad, I have to move on. I don't need you to protect me anymore. Jesus will protect me."

My father crouched back and said, "Don't say that name."

I realised that this wasn't my father. This was a spirit. It didn't want me to forgive. It didn't want me to move forward. It came in the appearance of one who could protect.

I looked past the spirit and saw my father standing just inside the door of the old house.

"Dad," I said. "I forgive you. I can't stay in this place anymore, but I forgive you."

Dad came out of the house and walked with me down to the car.

"Why don't you come with me Dad?" I asked him.

"We don't belong here."

Dad shook his head and I gave him a hug before I got in the car.

When I was seated, the car pulled away from the curb and drove down the street. I could see my father standing on the sidewalk, the house and his image growing smaller in the rear view mirror. I saw the house suddenly erupt in flames.

That was the end of that part of my life. There was no going back there now; there was nothing to go back to. I felt the Father whisper to me, "That's true forgiveness son. It's when there's nothing to go back to. It's how you've been forgiven."

I knew then that I was free to forgive anyone in the same manner. And so I did.

There is still more freedom that I am coming into. There are things that get exposed through situations. Tania can see it because my face changes. It looks like my eyes, nose and mouth squash together and are too small for my head. Tania says I look like a hawk (or a vulture) when it happens. I am learning to tell how it feels and, instead of denying it, I'll start to seek God and find out what is happening.

To be honest, it was only when God allowed me to see what I was doing to my family that I really got serious about being set free. I wanted some of the behaviours to stop, but a lot of the time, I didn't see it as my fault.

I felt that if my family could just see things from my perspective, they would understand that they were in the wrong, and they shouldn't do the things they had. I couldn't see there was something wrong with me and the way I related to my family. I couldn't see it was my fault and that I needed to change. But I did need to change and God intervened supernaturally, setting me free.

PART 11 – CHANGES

CHAPTER 45

Below is a list of some of the changes I have experienced since I received healing. It took me a while to notice some of these things, while others I noticed straight away. For me the biggest testimony is the fact that my wife can notice the difference.

One example of that is with conferences. My wife would suffer with anxiety leading up to and during conferences, because she didn't know when I was going to have a meltdown. She wouldn't know how badly she would be hurt attending the conference with me.

The last conference we went to, I was in better shape than she was during it. Even though we didn't get the kind of sleep I had needed in the past, I was more calm and relaxed than Tania. I was comfortable talking to people I didn't know and I didn't need my scripts. I had no meltdowns and I could actually lend strength to Tania to help her get through.

While conference was on, I was also organising paperwork for a building project. Some of the paperwork couldn't be found on the internet where it was supposed to be so I was making phone calls to get people organized to get the paperwork that was needed. It finally got up on the net the day before the project started and I was able to get it to the right people just in time.

I notice now that I can feel the cold. I could feel it before, but I didn't recognise what I was feeling as being cold. I would sleep in shorts and a t-shirt through winter and Tania would often tell me in the morning that my arm felt like ice, like it was dead.

Now through the night in winter if my arm is out of my blankets, it will wake me up. I will have to put it under the blankets because of how cold it is.

Tania now also doesn't feel like she is at a disadvantage if we have a cold feet and hand fight under the blankets at night.

A couple of years ago, Tania and I went to tea with some of our family and their friends. I looked uncomfortable after a while and Tania asked me what was wrong. I told her what was being said in every conversation around the room. I wasn't deliberately eavesdropping, I was just in a high state of anxiety and I couldn't filter out the conversations.

Not long after healing and deliverance, we were having lunch in the café at our church after the service. There was a lot of noise as there were quite a few people talking.

Tania turned to me from another table to talk to me. She had apparently been talking about me to the other people at her table and she asked me to clarify something she said. She had assumed I had heard the whole conversation but I hadn't.

I had heard my name when it was spoken but I didn't pay any more attention to the conversation. I assumed that if Tania wanted me to know what she was talking about she would tell me but until then it wasn't my business so the conversation was filtered out. I am sure this is a result of healing and deliverance in the area of ego-centricity as well as hypersensitivity.

I can experience empathy. I had not been able to do that before. I may have been able to guess what someone could be feeling based on what others had told me or what I had experienced, but I wouldn't know for sure.

True empathy is being able to feel how someone is feeling from their perspective and not your own. I was in a situation where someone was speaking about a certain thing and the facts they said were wrong.

In the past I would have corrected them because they were wrong, and also because what they had said put me in a bad light. Instead I stayed quiet and a short while later I just knew that the person was feeling insecure and what they said was to establish a sense of authority for themselves. They were not running me down or making me look bad. In fact it had nothing to do with me. That was the first time I had experienced true empathy.

I felt satisfaction from mowing the lawns for the first time in my life. In the past, I had always mown the lawns in anger. I had of course blamed my parents for that because they had made me mow lawns when I was younger. I had to mow a one acre block with a push motor mower regularly and it took a long time.

In truth, I was angry because it was an inconvenience. It was stopping me from doing whatever I wanted to do. When I lived with my parents I had to mow for them and now I was married I had to do it for my wife. It was their fault I wasn't getting to do what I liked. Tania felt that I was angry at her whenever I mowed the lawns, because I always looked angry. I probably was but I wouldn't admit it.

Everything I did around the house I saw as a duty and derived no pleasure from it. I said I did it all for Tania, but it was all done with a bad attitude so Tania never felt love from what I did.

After prayer, when I mowed the lawns I could stop after I had finished and admire them. I could be proud of the effort and the results. I began to see similar changes when I did other things around the house too.

I have been able to see when I am in the wrong. Where before I would argue and shift blame, I am able to admit fault and do what I need to make it right. This ties in closely with a new ability to be vulnerable to Tania and to emotionally connect with her.

This vulnerability has meant that changes have occurred in the bedroom. I am more willing to talk to Tania about love making and even ask her to make love. I wouldn't say anything before, just assuming that she would know what I was thinking. It has meant I am more in touch with her emotions as well as mine and I am more able to express the passion I feel for my wife.

It also means I won't sulk for weeks on end if I've done something wrong or if I feel I've been wronged. I'm not saying I now get it right all the time, because I don't, but I'm a lot better than I used to be.

One of the strangest feelings I'm getting used to is experiencing multiple emotions at the same time.

Not so long ago Caleb used a lot of extra time on the internet and the phone and it cost us an extra $300 on the phone bill. I was angry with him and in the past, when I dealt with him, that would be the only emotion I experienced. There would be no tempering of the anger with love. That didn't happen this time.

I sat down with him and talked to him about it calmly. I let him know how to tell he had gone over his internet limit. He then told me he saw the messages but didn't know what they meant. I knew he hadn't done this on purpose. I asked him what he could do so he could pay the money off. He knew he had done the wrong thing and he wanted to fix it. He suggested he could do extra chores around the house. I agreed with that and hugged him and it was all good.

I wasn't hiding my anger, or the disappointment I felt; it was just overwhelmed with love and understanding.

Not long after I noticed that Caleb was reacting badly to certain situations. I suddenly knew that the pressure of this debt was too much for him. I hadn't said anything more about it, and I hadn't put pressure on him to have to pay it but he was feeling it. He wasn't trying to get out of it either; it was just that the pressure of it was too much for him.

I went into his room with him and lay on the bed next to him and told him I released him from all the debt and we would never mention it again. Our twelve year old son rolled over and hugged me as tears ran down his face.

Before I was healed and delivered the results of this incident would have been completely different. I would have reacted out of anger and there would have been a harsh punishment.

I would not have seen the effect the pressure of the situation was having on Caleb and I never would have extended grace. He had done the crime and so punishment had to be carried out. If that didn't happen, then he would never learn and he would repeat the behaviour time and again.

I believe that my previous behaviour would have driven a wedge between Caleb and me that would have required a lot of undoing. I am sure that my actions in the past in regards to discipline with the girls caused wedges to form. I'm glad I've had the opportunity to apologise to them for what I had done.

The funny thing is that Caleb seems less inclined to repeat his behaviour with the phones than any other behaviour I have punished harshly. There's a lot to be said for the effects of grace.

Tania is less worried now when I get up to preach. She had been concerned that I would say something inappropriate or speak in a manner that was out of line. I find it easier to preach as well. I am more comfortable with words moving straight from my heart and out of my mouth. I would often rely solely on what I had written and that would stifle the Holy Spirit. My preaching has much more life in it now, than it did before I was set free.

Another important aspect of my freedom is an ability to adapt to situations quickly. In the past, if an emergency situation arose, and I was in "default mode," I would freeze. I wouldn't know what to do. I couldn't change my mental boxes fast enough.

Just recently, we had an incident outside our church. Caleb told me that there was a fight outside the church between some people. None of them were from the church. I went out to see if I could break it up.

I was very tense, with the possibility I might face violence myself. In the past, this would have caused me to go into "default mode."

When I went out, I found that one of the young men had been hit in the head with something and he was bleeding profusely. Instead of freezing, I organised people to get a cloth to put over the wound, a blanket for warmth and other things that were needed to look after him. I called the ambulance and then talked with the victim to keep him calm.

It surprised me how I responded to that situation. I was very happy with the change as well. I know God has done an amazing healing and deliverance in my life to set me free from Asperger's.

EPILOGUE

The following descriptions are based on actual events. I encountered this same situation before being set free from Asperger's and afterwards. The contrast between my responses is, to me, evidence of the healing and delivering work of Jesus Christ.

Before Healing and Deliverance :

It is Tuesday night and I have to take these DVDs back. They were supposed to be taken back this morning but they weren't because I was running late getting Caleb to school and that meant I was going to be late for work. I hated being late so I didn't stop to put the DVDs in.

I was late because Tania wanted to talk to me this morning about some dream she had. Why couldn't she just wait until later in the day? Now the DVDs are going to be late and I'll have to pay for it.

I walk into the store and someone is standing in front of the return slot. What do I do? I freeze while I think about it. Has this happened before? If it has, what did I do? Did it work or not? What was the result? If I haven't done this before, have I seen someone else encounter it? What did they do? Anxiety fills me. I start to shake a little because adrenaline floods my body preparing my fight or flight response.

I hadn't prepared for someone to be standing in front of the return slot. It threw out my plan. Now I will have to say something. What if I say something wrong? My body goes stiff as I walk to the slot, my gait becomes awkward. What if they ask me a question and I don't know what to say?

The flight or fight response takes over and when I get to the slot I say "Excuse me." But it comes out roughly. My face has gone blank or it's frowning because I'm concentrating so hard on what might happen. I've forgotten to smile.

The lady hears my tone and sees my face and quickly moves out of the way with an apology. To her I'm a big, angry, frightening man. I put the DVDs in hoping I don't miss the slot and drop them on the ground.

I turn and walk stiffly out of the shop, get into the car and start breathing again. I slow my breathing down and try to relax. It's OK now, it's all over.

I can't believe Tania made me late. I won't listen next time she tries to tell me a dream on a Tuesday morning.

After Healing and Deliverance:

It is Tuesday night and I'm returning the DVDs we had watched for family night the night before. I'm thinking about the good time I had with my family.

There's no concern about it being late, and even if it is, there's no blame for not getting it in there in the morning. It was a decision I made and what's more I was glad I could take the time to listen to

Tania share her dream and through that, her heart. I was glad I had a wife who loves me like she does.

I walk into the store to place the DVDs in the return slot and a lady is standing in front of it. I haven't planned my stop at the shop and seeing someone in front of the slot doesn't throw me. I don't need a script and when I say excuse me, it is with a light tone and the lady isn't frightened.

The lady moves and smiles and I put the DVDs in the slot. There's no adrenaline, no flight or fight, no anxiety.

I walk back to the car and get in. I sit, reflecting on the change and I noticed something else. My face had felt strange walking out of the shop. I didn't think about it or even realise it. I had just done it automatically. I had been smiling.

www.ingramcontent.com/pod-product-compliance
Lightning Source LLC
Chambersburg PA
CBHW060925040426
42445CB00011B/791